Dr. Philip Yeung takes the readers on a heart-searching discovery journey on the biblical meaning of calling. This scholarly exploration of the different Bible characters reveals calling as a gift to be received with our God-given identity, despite all our faults, weaknesses, and struggles, and is based on a living dynamic relationship with God. Calling comes to ordinary lives through the eyes of an extraordinary God. Even in apparent silence, God is at work. This book challenges our assumptions and priorities about calling, as following the Kingdom of God is just as important as proclaiming the Kingdom of God. This book was written out of a profound passion to apply biblical truths to real-life situations with a shepherding heart, helping readers to appreciate the sacredness of calling. This book is not for the faint-hearted but for anyone serious about finding their true identity and God's purpose for their lives.

Rev. Dr. Patrick Fung
Global Ambassador, OMF International;
International Board Chair, CCCOWE

Rev. Yeung's exposition on calling is pioneering for the Chinese church community. Calling is related to our personhood in God's image. It is about who we are, rather than what we are doing. I am so thankful for my learning from Rev. Yeung, from days of campus fellowship to seminary training. His teaching has helped me fundamentally to learn how to serve God with both fullness and gladness in my life.

Barry Cheung
General Secretary, Fellowship of Evangelical Students (FES) Hong Kong

Dr. Yeung leads us on a powerful and persuasive journey in *Calling: How the Bible draws the line between true and false calling*. The focus on Scripture and its context in order to help us discern our calling is so well done. I found the book to be challenging and convicting as well as life giving. Whether you are on a path towards vocational ministry or just wondering about God's calling in your life, this is a must read.

Alan Williams
Marketplace Ministries, Pioneers Europe

The concept of calling might sound esoteric, but in reality, God extends a universal calling to every individual from the moment of their birth. This universal calling entails living a life of abundance, embracing and delighting in His love, and partnering with Him in the stewardship of the Earth to bring glory to His name. Additionally, in different periods of time, God bestows upon some individuals a specific calling, a mission that goes beyond the universal calling. I am grateful for Dr. Yeung's book, *Calling*, for its vivid and lucid exploration of both the universal and specific dimensions of calling. This book not only helps us appreciate the wonder of God's calling but also serves as a reminder that living a life pleasing to God isn't about pursuing the 'halo' of having a special calling. Instead, it's about humbly embracing the life that God has bestowed upon us, especially for those of us who have a specific vocation. Regardless of the calling we have received from God, we are all created to respond to His calling with the entirety of our lives.

Rev. Kam Wong Ng
Secretary General, Hong Kong Alliance Mission

This book is an innovative, comprehensive guide to discern God's calling in your life journey. It explains clearly the meaning of calling, and illustrates with concrete models from the Bible ways to live out a called life. The exposition is intriguingly intertwined with Biblical truth and the pastoral heart of Dr. Yeung, the author.

Dr. Jimmy Man
Vice President, Evangel Seminary, Hong Kong

The original Chinese book *Calling* by the late Dr. Yeung has been transforming countless disciples in the Chinese church community. I believe that the English translated version by Dr. Yeung's family will have the same impact on disciples in the Western world. The book is a profound exploration of the genuine biblical meaning of our individual callings in a unique fashion by Dr. Yeung, who had been coaching us with a fatherly heart. "A calling is a burden, it is seeing a need — not from a human perspective, but from God's perspective ..." These are the words that have inspired me a lot. I pray that this remarkable book will transcend generations, offering timeless principles to inspire and shape the readers.

Dr. K. K. Liu
Private Anaesthesiologist; Layman leader and disciple maker in the ministry of Faculty of Medicine, HKU

DR. PHILIP YEUNG

Calling

How the Bible draws the line between true and false calling

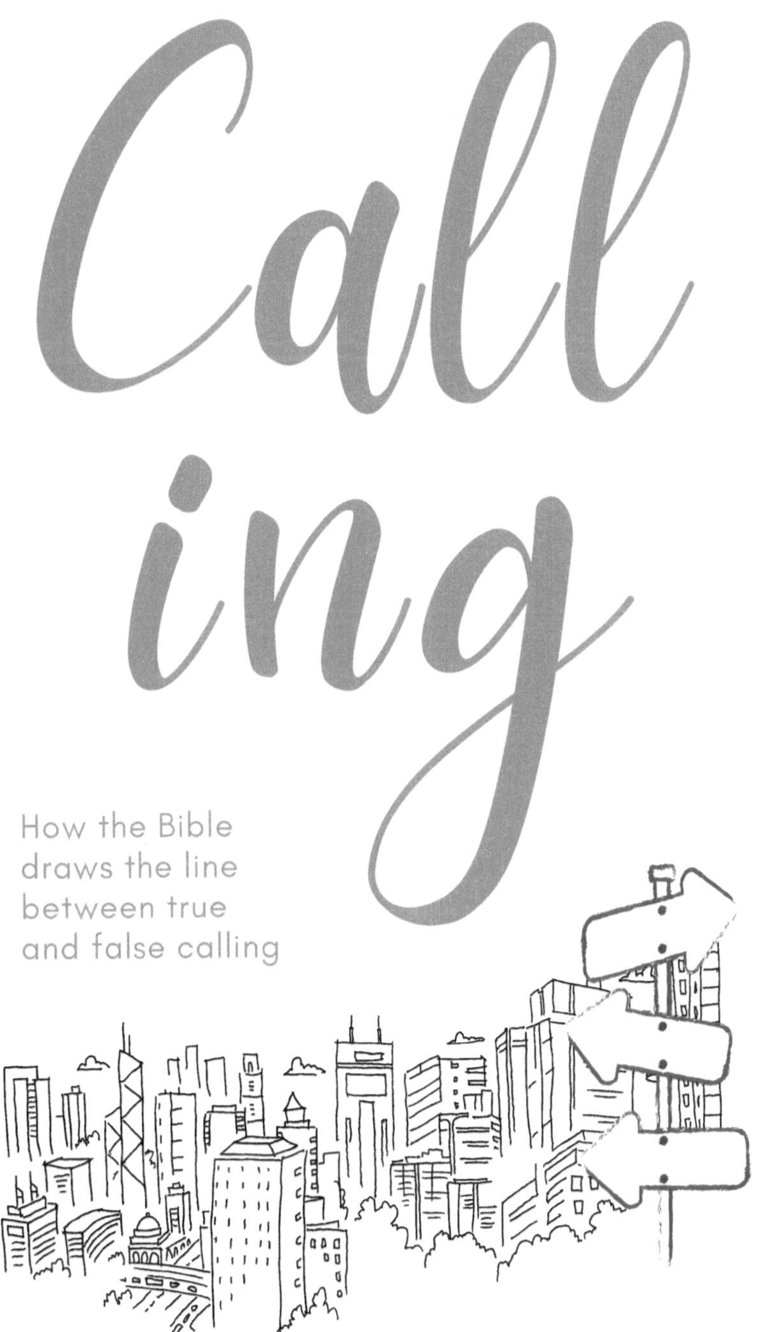

First published by Yeung E Publishing 2023

Translation & editing: Joanie Yeung
Editing & proofreading: Aimee Williams, Stella Yeung
Cover design: Joanie Yeung / Canva.com

Cataloguing-in-Publication data: Name: Yeung, Philip. [author] Title: Calling: how the Bible draws the line between true and false calling / Philip Yeung. LCSH: Vocation—Christianity. Discipling (Christianity). Christian life. Work—Religious aspects—Christianity
BV4740 Y364 2024
Dewey class no. 248.4

First edition

This book was professionally typeset on Reedsy.

ISBN:
9798224363223 (eBook)
9798224184583 (paperback)
9798882709593 (hardcover)

To all who are created in His image

Contents

Editor's Note & Acknowledgements

This book is a compilation of talks, course materials and sermons by my late father Dr Philip Yeung on the topic of God's calling, a biblical theme that was central to his teachings and ministries throughout his 40 years of teaching at China Graduate School of Theology (CGST) and pastoring at the Emmanuel Chinese Church in Kowloon, Hong Kong. After his passing in 2020 after a battle with pancreatic cancer, friends and family have started a publication project to collect and publish his works, as well as translating some of them into English so they may reach a wider audience.

Most of the chapters in this book originate from a course he taught at CGST between 1996 until his retirement in 2013. This course was especially designed to equip Christians engaged in the marketplace and those contemplating a full-time ministry vocation, providing them with a robust biblical foundation for discerning God's calling in their lives and engaging in deeper introspection on their walk with God.

In 2017, CGST compiled the course materials into Chinese and published *Answering His Call* (ISBN: 9789887768265). Among the various books derived from Dr Yeung's teachings on God's calling, this particular volume stands out for its comprehensiveness on the topic of God's calling.

In early 2023, my family obtained permission from CGST to undertake the task of translating and publishing this book in English. However, given the fact that English writing takes up much more space than Chinese characters, a direct, literal translation would produce an English book of more than 1,000 pages. We have therefore made some adaptations, omitted a couple of overlapping chapters already published in other English publications, and with the kind permission of Emmanuel Chinese Church, incorporated a couple of relevant Sunday sermons that also pertained to the subject of calling. We have also decided to publish the chapters on Sabbath in a separate volume in the future.

I would like to express my heartfelt gratitude to CGST for their gracious permission for me to translate into English this collection of materials on the course Discipleship, Calling and Life, making it accessible to non-Chinese readers and allowing it to be translated into other languages in the future. This translation and publication project is also indebted to the generosity of Emmanuel Chinese Church, Hong Kong, who has made Dr Yeung's sermons and talks widely and freely accessible online.

Finally, I am also deeply grateful to many loving family members and friends for their continuous encouragement and support throughout this challenging yet rewarding publication journey.

Joanie Yeung

Preface

The concept of calling is fundamental in our Christian faith. Transcending far beyond simply the choice of career paths or ministry roles, it encompasses every facet of our lives. I believe a comprehensive biblical view of calling is to be seen through the lens of creation: God inscribed the names of individuals He intended to create in heaven even before the world's formation. Then He calls them to live out the purpose He designed for them. God calls, and we respond with our entire lives – this, in essence, is calling.

The understanding of calling has been a crucial foundation and milestone in my personal spiritual journey. Despite growing up in a Christian environment and being active in church and fellowship from a young age, the concept of calling remained conspicuously absent from my upbringing. No one ever mentioned to me the concept of calling or provided teachings on its meaning. As I embarked on my university education, I naturally embraced the conventional aspirations of most young people, pursuing my career and envisioning my future with worldly values.

My world was completely changed when I attended a summer camp organised by one of the university Christian fellowships under the Fellowship of Evangelical Students (FES). There, I came to recognise that we are uniquely created and called to live out a divine purpose entrusted by the Lord. This revelation changed my life trajectory. I realised that I should no longer live for myself but solely for the Lord.

Eventually, due to the burden placed on my heart by the Lord, I made the life-changing decision to leave behind my medical profession to fully commit myself to the ministry of biblical education. The biblical understanding of calling has had a tremendous impact on my life. It not only shaped my entire life journey, it has also been the central message in my teachings and pastoral work.

Starting from 1996, at the China Graduate School of Theology where I taught, we collaborated with FES's Graduate Christian Fellowship to offer an evening Christian Studies Diploma programme. Central to this programme was a mandatory course titled "Discipleship, Calling and Life". Since then, I have had the privilege of teaching this vital subject to many Christians and seminary students. This book is a collection of the teaching materials and discussions on calling I have developed in this course over the years.

The primary goal of the course "Discipleship, Calling and Life" is not to provide students with careers advice or practical formulae for discovering one's calling. It is to equip students to reflect and discern God's plan for them with a solid biblical foundation, stimulating students to re-examine both Scripture and their own lives continuously and deeply, living out a fruitful life as disciples of Christ.

Therefore, both the course itself and the content within this book are intentionally devoid of rigid, one-size-fits-all systems. Discussions about calling, much like the rich tapestry of biblical teachings, cannot be neatly reduced to a checklist or a set formula. Indeed, each person's calling is intricately linked to their specific circumstances in different phases of their lives. The understanding and realisation of God's calling are by no means limited to cognitive recognition within the mind; it further involves continuous introspection, reflection, and at times, even different struggles in real life.

This book begins by introducing some essential biblical concepts related to calling, emphasising its sacredness and the importance of a sense of calling for all believers. Many of the biblical stories examined in this book reveal the intricate deceptions that cloud the human heart, preventing many from living out the true self that is created by God. These factors include the pressures and allures from the world, false expectations, self-righteousness, and a reluctant heart to fully obey. As Jesus's call to deny ourselves, take up our cross and follow him stands as the cornerstone of our calling in the New Testament, the book concludes with a deeper examination of the essence of discipleship as told in the Gospels.

I am most grateful to my Heavenly Father who created and called me. He instilled in my heart a profound passion for biblical education early on, granted me the ability and gifts to live out this calling, and bestowed abundant grace upon me during difficult times. My journey also includes my wife, Stella, who understands, accompanies, and fully supports my ministry. She has played a vital role in the shaping, growth and the building up of my life and is an indispensable part of my journey.

With a heart full of gratitude to the Heavenly Father, I offer this book as a fragrant offering, praying that God will use His Word to bring blessings to many.

Philip Yeung
(2017)

I

What really 'drives' you?

Being driven by a 'false calling'

1

Esau

This book explores the true meaning of calling and examines how discerning and living out God's calling is demonstrated practically in the Bible. Abundant with both positive and negative examples of people responding to God's calling, the Bible serves as a rich source of guidance for our life journey. Let's embark on this journey by examining the sobering story of Esau in Genesis. Esau's loss of his birthright, though heart-wrenching, offers valuable insights into how we might easily and carelessly overlook fundamental aspects of God's calling in our lives. His story serves as a poignant wakeup call for us all.

How could anyone lose his birthright status? In ancient societies, a firstborn son automatically received the birthright. The birthright was a sacred calling that represented privileges, blessings and the continuation of God's covenant with His people. However, the Bible shows us that losing one's birthright is not only possible, it can happen fairly easily.

Let's begin by looking at Genesis 25:21–23:

> 21 Isaac prayed to the Lord on behalf of his wife, because she was childless. The Lord answered his prayer, and his wife Rebekah became pregnant. 22 The babies jostled each other within her, and she said, "Why is this happening to me?" So she went to enquire

> of the Lord. ²³ The Lord said to her, "Two nations are in your womb, and two peoples from within you will be separated; one people will be stronger than the other, and the elder will serve the younger."

Are we the product of our family circumstances or God's master plan?

Let's examine the background of the story. When Rebekah cast her burden on God, God showed her the future of her two children. As a mother-to-be, Rebekah probably wondered, "Why does God have to make things so complicated?" but she must also have been comforted that God planned to give her twins!

The passage makes it clear that God knew every aspect of the sons' lives even before they were born. The same is true in our lives. Like an architect who prepares a blueprint before the construction of a building, or a knitter who has a pattern and colours in mind before knitting a sweater, God has a clear plan for who He wants to create and call us to be. This is a powerful reminder of the sovereignty of God's creation.

Verses 24–27 continue:

> ²⁴ When the time came for her to give birth, there were twin boys in her womb. ²⁵ The first to come out was red, and his whole body was like a hairy garment; so they named him Esau. ²⁶ After this, his brother came out, with his hand grasping Esau's heel; so he was named Jacob. Isaac was sixty years old when Rebekah gave birth to them. ²⁷ The boys grew up, and Esau became a skilful hunter, a man of the open country, while Jacob was content to stay at home among the tents.

Although the two brothers were twins, their personalities, temperaments, passions and gifts couldn't have been more different. One loved being at home, the other went out hunting all day. An unfortunate difference between the two brothers, however, was evident not in the contrast in their hobbies and appearances, but elsewhere. The next verse says: "Isaac, who had a taste for wild game, loved Esau, but Rebekah loved Jacob" (v. 28).

This caused bitterness and rivalry between Esau and Jacob, which led to disputes and tragedy. Yet, despite the unfortunate circumstances, God used the rivalry between them to fulfil His plan.

Our family of origin is an integral factor that shapes who we are today. Sadly, some families can be unhealthy, hurtful or even dysfunctional. Rather than trying to deny this fact, complain about it or place blame on others, we are called to face the reality of our family of origin with courage and faith. God knew the profound influences that our families and upbringing could have on each of us before we were even born. In fact, He orchestrated every detail to work out His plan and calling for us.

When we review our life journey from birth to the present, including all the ups and downs in our childhood, relationships and career paths, many of us recognise that there were times when we were harmed by the wrongdoings of other people. It is natural to feel like blaming, complaining and questioning why a loving God would allow us to go through such pain. We look back and can't help but feel angry and hurt. We wonder why we had to suffer because of the selfish choices of others.

In God's creation, there is no need to fear, worry or be hindered by external circumstances in our lives. God not only knows all these factors, He works wonders with them. God has already taken into account even the worst of situations and painful experiences and He desires to transform them into blessings. Difficult circumstances can be in fact part of our calling.

The story of the two brothers continues. Verses 29–34 tell us:

> [29] Once when Jacob was cooking some stew, Esau came in from the open country, famished. [30] He said to Jacob, "Quick, let me have some of that red stew! I'm famished!" (That is why he was also called Edom.)

> **31** Jacob replied, "First sell me your birthright."
>
> **32** "Look, I am about to die," Esau said. "What good is the birthright to me?"
>
> **33** But Jacob said, "Swear to me first." So he swore an oath to him, selling his birthright to Jacob.
>
> **34** Then Jacob gave Esau some bread and some lentil stew. He ate and drank, and then got up and left. So Esau despised his birthright.

Esau's decision to give up his birthright carries the utmost significance and enduring consequences. In ancient Hebrew culture, the birthright was a position of immense privilege and responsibility. It meant not only a double portion of the family's inheritance but also the spiritual leadership of the family, carrying on God's everlasting covenant with Abraham. Forsaking it would be a grave disregard for the sacredness of his birthright and all the blessings that came with it. Esau was forfeiting his everlasting leadership role in carrying God's blessings for the family line, bestowed upon him as the eldest son. This effectively ruined not only his personal destiny but also the destiny of all his descendants, both physically and spiritually.

How did this tragedy all begin?

Esau's life was centred around pleasing someone (his father). This was his self-given identity, his source of purpose, self-worth and recognition. However, it was not the identity bestowed upon him by God, and Esau wore himself out chasing after this false calling. Isn't this the life lived by many Christians today? Life is a stressful, relentless pursuit. With costs of living rising faster than our salaries, we may find ourselves struggling to make ends meet. Many of us resemble Esau, racing through life and meeting different expectations with little time to contemplate something as abstract as 'God's calling.' Exhausted people often lack the mental or physical capacity to consider God's plan. It's crucial to pause and ask ourselves: Is this our reality? Are we, too, succumbing to fatigue, like Esau?

Let us consider Esau's condition. First, he stated that he was desperately worn out and "about to die" (v. 32). But was he *really* going to die? Should

Jacob have called an ambulance or prepared to perform CPR? The Bible tells us that after accepting Jacob's deal and taking some stew, Esau simply got up and left (v. 34), as if nothing had happened. One can safely conclude that Esau didn't have any urgent medical needs, nor was he in danger of dying. Esau was simply exaggerating his feelings at the time.

Our priorities in life shape our sense of reality and the magnitude of the problems we experience. If we believe something is trivial, then its absence isn't an issue. But if we believe something is vital, then its absence poses a massive problem for us. Why was Esau callous about his birthright? The story doesn't give us an indication that the family was in need; there's also no hint of hunger or poverty in their story. So, a critical question is: Why was Esau so exhausted from his hunting that he felt he was dying?

The true drive behind Esau's actions

Esau was a wild hunter who loved his father, and his hunting talent was indeed a gift from God. What's wrong with incorporating your passion into your work while serving your family? Nothing. There is nothing wrong with providing food for your parents while doing what you enjoy.

However, Esau was compelled to hunt frenetically by a powerful force – a longing, or a *drive*. We can understand the root of this longing. Rebekah favoured the younger twin Jacob, and Esau knew that no matter what he did, he would never win his mother's favour. Only his father valued and appreciated him, so he devoted himself to pleasing Isaac by hunting endlessly to make up for the lack of maternal love and to secure his place in his father's heart. This was Esau's *drive*, but this was not God's *calling*.

Drive is the opposite of calling. It is something God never calls us to pursue, and as a result, it is a longing that can never be satisfied. Drives often lead to burnout, and being burned out is never part of God's calling – He's the God of the Sabbath. Living out God's calling may keep us busy and occupied, but it will never lead to burnout. On the contrary, doing what God has called us to do will lead to joy and satisfaction.

Imagine you have a car with a broken engine. You must get out and push it from behind. After pushing the car just a few metres you will be exhausted. But once the engine is properly restored, with just a gentle pressure on the gas pedal, the car will run effortlessly, powered by its own engine.

Sometimes, a drive and a calling may appear the same on the outside. But there is always a fine line between them. A particular activity might represent a calling, or it might betray a drive. God might well have called Esau to serve his family with his hunting skills. Yet once Esau saw hunting as his source of security, purpose and identity, he lost his true identity. We might be doing what God has called us to do, but once we inject our own drives and false identities into it to satisfy our unfulfilled needs, our work becomes a black hole sucking away our God-given life, blurring our sight and blinding us to our true calling.

Is it a calling from God or a drive from the world?

Our value system says a lot about our spiritual condition, and vice versa. We all have desires, longings and motivations behind everything we do. We may like to believe our actions are driven by a higher calling, but in reality, in our hearts, we desire approval, praise and recognition from others. None of these is God's calling.

Let's ask ourselves some sobering questions. Have we mixed other drives into our appearance of living out God's calling? Are we really following God or are we following our own desires? God is the only one who gives us the fulfilment and meaning that we seek. When we seek fulfilment and meaning from any other source, we are living Esau's life, regardless of how noble our actions may appear to others.

Some people may interpret Esau's decision to prioritize physical food over his birthright as a simple choice between the worldly and the spiritual. However, Esau's story is much more far-reaching and tragic than a mere conflict between the secular and the sacred. The type or nature of an activity is not what makes it worldly. 'Worldly' is not the opposite of 'spiritual', but rather the opposite of 'holy'. Holiness is more than simply the absence of sin; it is being set apart. God is holy, which means that God is set apart from everything else. Anything that belongs to God, whether it appears to be 'spiritual' or not, must be set apart from others for God.

Herein lies the true essence of calling: God has chosen you, set you apart from the world, redeemed you with a steep price and called you to be the person He has created you to be. Just as God called Abraham, Isaac and Jacob to form the nation of God's chosen people, you are called to be His people. If you choose to devote your life to pursue other things – no matter how beneficial or noble – you are going down the wrong path.

Therefore, in contemplating our vocations as God's calling, Christians must not simplistically label vocations such as pastor, evangelist or missionary as 'sacred', but regard business, banking or real estate (or as in Esau's case, hunting) as 'worldly', while considering social work, medicine or teaching as somewhere in the middle. This is not how God categorises vocations. What matters to God is whether we are being the people God has created us to be or if we are striving to be someone we were never meant to be.

The essence of being chosen

A firstborn is a firstborn. The Bible does not actually provide any task lists or instruction manuals for firstborns to follow. All they need to do is to receive their blessings and inheritance when the time comes. Their identity is a bestowed gift from birth that cannot be earned.

Being the firstborn is not a job to do, an achievement to attain, a puzzle to figure out or a lost item to find. The same is true of God's calling for each of us today. But don't these descriptions depict our everyday lives? Many Christians tell me they are trying very hard to *find* their calling or *figure out* what God wants them to do. As far as Esau's story was concerned, there was nothing for Esau to find or figure out throughout his life. He only needed to *be* the firstborn and not give up his God-given identity! Sadly, he found something else – hunting to please his father – and it became his pseudo-calling. Ironically, his father eventually failed him and gave his blessings to his brother Jacob.

Tragically, likewise, many Christians exhaust themselves through *doing* something, rather than *receiving* God's blessings and *being* who God has created and called them to be. Scripture says Esau "despised" his birthright (v. 34). What a tragic word to describe his attitude towards his true identity and calling! His biggest gift and calling from God had become so trivial in his eyes that Jacob's stew was more important.

An integral part of discerning one's calling is *listening*. When God calls, listen very carefully. However, it's important to understand that listening doesn't entail passively waiting for a divine instruction manual to descend from the heavens or for a mystical voice to speak. Instead, through reading and applying His Word, it involves discerning what truly matters to God and distinguishing between what holds significance and what does not. The deeper our understanding of God's heart, the clearer our own calling becomes. Only then can we watch out for drives and pursuits that are not part of God's calling.

God's sovereignty determines what holds true significance in our lives, yet the choice of what we value or despise lies with us. We can ask ourselves: What do we truly value, and what do we despise? Our calling is essentially a free gift to be received and an identity to be lived out in faith. It is not something to be hunted and pursued tirelessly. It is about *being*, not *doing*. From birth, Esau had already been given the most precious gift by his Heavenly Father. Yet he wore himself out by trying to earn the approval of his earthly father, and in the process, he lost his most valuable asset forever. God has created each person with a purpose and calling. The key is how we see and value this gift.

2

Martha

Busy, busy, busy. Is there a Christian today who doesn't have a busy life? I hardly know any.

The Bible never directly condemns being busy as bad or sinful, but it does have some sobering reminders for us. While in the Old Testament, we can learn about Esau's tragic story of trading off his precious birthright in the midst of exhaustion, there is an interestingly comparable story in the New Testament: the story of Martha and Mary recorded in Luke 10.

Indeed, Martha's problem seems to be of much lesser magnitude when compared to Esau's fate of losing his birthright and blessings forever. But when you compare the two, they are strangely similar. These stories are not just about sibling rivalries. Both Esau and Martha lost sight of something precious to them because they were occupied by something else.

Let's read Martha's story in Luke 10:38–42 (ESV):

> 38 Now as they went on their way, Jesus entered a village. And a woman named Martha welcomed him into her house. 39 And she had a sister called Mary, who sat at the Lord's feet and listened to his teaching. 40 But Martha was distracted with much serving. And she went up to him and said, "Lord, do you not care that my sister has left me to serve alone? Tell her then to help me." 41 But

> the Lord answered her, "Martha, Martha, you are anxious and troubled about many things, [42] but one thing is necessary. Mary has chosen the good portion, which will not be taken away from her."

A short story that is not as simple as it seems

Many Christians are familiar with this story, but often with several preconceived assumptions. It is easy to conclude that Jesus prefers us to be listening (like Mary) and dislikes us to be busy working (like Martha). This assumption may lead to a distorted way of dividing Christians into two types: one being busy with activities all day, and the other quietly seeking closeness with the Lord. We like to think the former is 'worldly', and the latter is 'spiritual', as if it is a distinction between right and wrong.

This classification is not fair. Martha welcomed Jesus and took him into her home, which was a noble thing to do at that time. To receive a rabbi and to serve him attentively was also a sacred service. Imagine if Martha had not taken up this task. Who would have served Jesus and the other guests? If everyone had sat down like Mary and just listened to Jesus's teachings, would the feast have been turned into a fast?

One thing readers of the story need to bear in mind when reading this story is that Jesus never criticised Martha for working in the kitchen and not sitting at his feet. Jesus was not the one criticising; Martha was. If Martha had refrained from complaining, this episode would not have happened at all.

Imagine if you were in Martha's shoes, facing a mountain of tasks to be completed. What would be your way out? This is the dilemma we all have to face today. Scripture shows us a contrast between the two sisters, but the contrast does not truly lie in the nature of their activities. The point of the story is *not* whose activity is more pleasing to God. If this is our conclusion, we haven't solved the problem. Someone still has to do the cooking and serve all the guests.

If Jesus wasn't saying that we should work less and do spiritual things more, then what is the story about?

Unmasking the truth about busyness

The story highlights a numerical contrast: Jesus said to Martha:

> "Martha, Martha, you are anxious and troubled about *many* things, but *one* thing is necessary." (vv. 41–42 ESV, emphasis added).

The obvious contrast is 'many' versus 'one'. If you read the passage carefully, you can see that every time the word 'many' appears, it is closely associated with something negative: "But Martha was distracted with *much* serving" (in v. 40, the original Greek word used is "many"); "you are anxious and troubled about *many* things" (v. 41).

Should Martha have cooked less for the guests? That would have meant less food to prepare, fewer plates to wash, and hence less stress for Martha! But is "many" the real root of the problem here? If you invite Jesus to your house for dinner, you wouldn't prepare just one dish, would you? So, doing many things (the quantity) is not necessarily the main issue Jesus wants to address.

We live in a world where multitasking is a survival skill. Everyone is multitasking. We can talk on the phone, reply to emails, have our meals and watch TV, all at the same time. Again, Jesus was not criticising Martha for having many things to do, but instead, he exposed the true condition of her heart: anxious and troubled. What made her so troubled and distracted?

Before we continue, I'd also like to draw attention to another common misunderstanding of this story. It is easy for readers to conclude that Mary's choice was better than Martha's. This is probably due to the familiar New International Version which translates Mary's choice as "what is better" (v. 42 NIV). However, the original Greek text does not have the word 'better'. The adjective used by Jesus is 'good'. Therefore, I've chosen to use the English Standard Version (ESV) for this passage, which renders verse 42 as "Mary has chosen the good portion." Jesus isn't making a comparison of which sister's activity is better, as modern readers have sometimes assumed. The moral of the story is *not* that cooking for Jesus is not as good as sitting near Jesus.

So, what exactly is the moral of the story, then? The clue is in the ending. Have you noticed the author has not given a specific ending to the story? We don't know Martha's reaction to Jesus's comments. The author seems to have ended the story abruptly on purpose. But why? Did Martha go back to the kitchen to cook? Or did she put down her apron and sit at Jesus's feet? Or did Mary get up and go help out in the kitchen? What exactly did Jesus want Martha to do next? The Bible doesn't tell us. Again, this shows that Jesus was not addressing a logistical problem. Jesus's answer to the question was not how the sisters should have taken turns or hired a kitchen helper, or how Martha should have balanced her life more effectively. No, nothing like that.

Very often, when a story in the Gospels ends abruptly, the last line reveals the most significant point of the story. In this case, it is Jesus's statement (v. 42):

> "Mary has chosen the good portion, which will not be taken away from her."

Mary had chosen something good which Martha had no right to take away.

The phrase "will not be taken away" is a profound reminder for us that we all have something in our lives that must be carefully guarded, given first priority, and which should never be taken away. We can apply this directly in our everyday life, in the sense that we have to intentionally choose the 'portion' in our lives that we cannot afford to lose, and know that other people must not be allowed to take it away from us. The book of Ecclesiastes consistently emphasises the importance of knowing and living out the portion given to us. For Esau, that should have been his birthright. Do we recognise our 'portion' in our lives that we must guard and treasure above all else?

The tyranny of the urgent and the power of choice

Today, many of us are facing what is called the tyranny of the urgent. We are like slaves to what appears to be urgent. Every day, we constantly feel compelled to attend to numerous time-sensitive matters that arise at home and at work. These tasks will never stop consuming our energy.

Urgent matters are not necessarily matters of great value. We must distinguish between the two. The most tragic thing that can happen to us is when these urgent matters of lesser value eventually take away what has eternal value. For example, spending time with God, reading Scripture and praying often seem to be the least urgent matters. We don't face immediate consequences when we delay doing these things. Sadly, our quality time with God is being squeezed out while life has many more urgent things we feel we must deal with.

You may wonder whether this is just a matter of priority. Of course, we all know we should put God first, but what is in second place after God? Is it family second, work or study third, and so on? Remember, God does not need to compete with other people or things at all. God is not an item on your to-do list. He is your Creator. He is the King in every realm. He calls us to love Him with all our heart, soul, mind and strength.

Let's go back to the text. The verb that Jesus uses when describing Mary's condition is 'to choose': "Mary has chosen the good portion." Once we identify what we must not lose, then we can *choose* to intentionally say "no" to things that are not part of the good portion from God, no matter how they beg for our attention. Every one of us has blessings and a unique calling from God. We must reflect carefully upon what the portion is that God has given us, the portion that can never be taken away, and then choose to guard it and focus on it. And once we have made that choice, then even the most hectic work schedule in the world will not turn us into Martha.

A professor once conducted an experiment with his students in class. He brought in a large tank, as well as an assortment of rocks, ranging from large to small, as well as sand. The goal is to fill the tank completely. The professor instructed the students to first place all the large rocks into the tank. "Is there still space?" he asked. The students replied, "Yes!" So, they added the smaller stones, filling the gaps. "Is there still space?" the professor inquired again. Although there wasn't much space left, they managed to pour in a significant amount of sand. After the students had added the sand, the professor asked, "Is there any space left now? Is the tank truly full?" The astute students realized the tank wasn't entirely full yet and quickly fetched several buckets of water, pouring them in until the tank was genuinely filled to capacity.

Gazing at the completely filled tank, the professor asked, "What lesson can we draw from this experiment?" The students responded, "We thought the space was already full, but it turns out there was still room for more." However, the professor clarified that this wasn't the primary lesson. The essential lesson was: You need to put the large rocks in first, then the smaller stones, followed by the sand, and finally, pour in the water. Only by following this sequence can everything fit. If you fill the tank with small pebbles and sand first, there won't be room for the large rocks.

Our issue often lies in letting small things take precedence, leaving no space for the important ones. This results in having no place for the big things and chaos with the small ones. Choose what's indispensable, and make space for them. This way, you'll find plenty of remaining space to accommodate other things.

I have a close friend who has a strong love for eating oysters. Since oysters are expensive, an all-you-can-eat buffet would be the best setting in which to consume them. My friend has developed a smart approach at buffets to maximise his enjoyment. He always makes sure he eats six oysters before going for other dishes. By doing so, he can fully indulge in his favourite food before he becomes filled with other things. This intentional decision to prioritise oysters allows him to relish every moment spent savouring them at a buffet.

Making a choice takes courage and willpower

Now, I'd like to draw your attention to another aspect of this story, one that is often overlooked by modern readers. Mary's choice of sitting at Jesus's feet was in no way easier than Martha's choice of serving in the kitchen. In fact, I'd argue that Mary's choice was much more challenging than Martha's. To understand why, we need to understand the social customs in Jesus's time.

The writer introduces Mary by saying that she "sat at the Lord's feet and listened to his teaching" (v. 39). In those days, only a rabbi's closest followers would sit in close proximity to the rabbi, and in first-century Palestine, they would certainly be 100% male. So, Mary wasn't just joining in for fun. She wasn't too lazy to help in the kitchen. Her action of sitting right at the feet of Jesus to listen to his teaching was an incredibly bold and intentional challenge to the social boundaries at the time. In doing so, Mary had to endure enormous pressure and scrutiny from all those around her, including her own sister and other religious leaders. In Martha's eyes, Mary wasn't in her right place. Martha might have been thinking, "Who do you think you are?"

Therefore, Mary's choice took a great deal of courage and deliberate thought. Choosing what cannot be taken away requires clear insights and an unwavering willpower to stick to it until the end.

Eugene H. Peterson, a pastor and renowned professor of contemporary spiritual theology, shared an experience that shed light on the idea of choosing the good portion. In 1962, Peterson was asked by his denomination, the Presbyterian Church USA, to establish a new church in Bel Air, Maryland. However, Peterson quickly realized that despite all his studies and experiences, the sheer volume of tasks before him were overwhelming. These demands compelled him to reconsider what a pastor's true calling was and determine if he was living up to his calling. He maintained that three things in a pastor's role can never be taken away: praying, learning God's

Word, and giving spiritual direction.[1] These three things remain essential, while all other things can be taken away if they interfere with the 'good portion'. Once he identified these three angles, as he called them, he was able to stay focused. Can we identify our 'good portion' amid never-ending errands and hectic schedules?

What is the good portion that God has given to you? Choose it, stick with it with boldness and determination, and it will not be taken away.

---

[1] Eugene Peterson, Working the Angles: The Shape of Pastoral Integrity. Eerdmans, 1987.

II

What are you doing here?

Shedding the layers of the false self

3

Elijah

Elijah, a renowned major prophet in the Old Testament, is often remembered as a tough and fearless figure who challenged the prophets of Baal. His dramatic showdown against Baal's prophets on Mount Carmel demonstrated his unwavering faith and God's power (1 Kings 18). Yet immediately afterwards, when Elijah heard that Jezebel was pursuing him, he fled for his life. We see a severely depressed, disillusioned, pathetic Elijah begging God to end his life! We sometimes forget that Elijah's life displayed both tremendous success and crushing failure.

As we examine the events from 1 Kings 18 onwards, it is clear that Elijah's burnout had only intensified. He even outran Ahab's chariot on a 25-mile journey from Mount Carmel to Jezreel (18:45–46). In 1 Kings 19, he had reached the end of ordinary human capacity:

> [1] Now Ahab told Jezebel everything Elijah had done and how he had killed all the prophets with the sword. [2] So Jezebel sent a messenger to Elijah to say, "May the gods deal with me, be it ever so severely, if by this time tomorrow I do not make your life like that of one of them." [3] Elijah was afraid and ran for his life. When he came to Beersheba in Judah, he left his servant there, [4] while he himself went a day's journey into the wilderness. He came to

> a broom bush, sat down under it and prayed that he might die. "I have had enough, Lord," he said. "Take my life; I am no better than my ancestors." **5** Then he lay down under the bush and fell asleep. All at once an angel touched him and said, "Get up and eat." **6** He looked around, and there by his head was some bread baked over hot coals, and a jar of water. He ate and drank and then lay down again. **7** The angel of the Lord came back a second time and touched him and said, "Get up and eat, for the journey is too much for you." **8** So he got up and ate and drank. Strengthened by that food, he traveled forty days and forty nights until he reached Horeb, the mountain of God. **9** There he went into a cave and spent the night. And the word of the Lord came to him: "What are you doing here, Elijah?"

To escape from Jezebel's daring death threat, Elijah ran almost 100 miles from Jezreel to Beersheba (19:3). Upon arrival, he walked in the wilderness for a day before collapsing in despair and wishing to die (19:4). Then he walked for another 40 days and nights to reach Mount Horeb, a distance of at least 200 miles (19:8). What exactly was Elijah doing?

At the heart of Elijah's emotional and spiritual burnout was a sense of false self, a façade that he adopted to meet the expectations of himself and others. In this chapter, we will explore the intriguing dialogue between Elijah and God in 1 Kings 19, reflecting on its valuable lessons for Christians struggling with the pressures of maintaining a false self and how God's grace and truth can turn our perspectives right side up again.

The reality of burnout

> "Take my life; I am no better than my ancestors." (1 Kings 19:4)

Elijah's plea was a plea to give up. For him, life was too much to bear. The angel later told him, "The journey is too much for you" (1 Kings 19:7), which meant there was even more to come. Elijah was overwhelmed by exhaustion and the desperation to end it all. It seemed that there was too much to do and too much to cope with.

Let's empathise with Elijah and put ourselves in his shoes. While he seemed confident during the fight on Mount Carmel, he was facing a life-or-death battle, and defeat would mean his death. Even without an immediate threat, he was already physically and mentally exhausted and on the verge of collapse. Compounding this was the fact that there were powerful people after his life, which added immense pressure to his already fragile state. Elijah wasn't just suffering from physical exhaustion; he was also facing prolonged psychological pressure that weighed him down.

Consider Elijah's plea for death. "Take my life", he said, "I am no better than my ancestors" (1 Kings 19:4). What did he mean by "no better than my ancestors"? He had just achieved a great victory over the prophets of Baal with an unprecedented display of spiritual power. Why was he now engulfed in despair? What was it about the previous prophets, his "ancestors", that made him feel inadequate in comparison?

Perhaps he was comparing himself with Moses, who demonstrated remarkable patience when leading the Israelites out of Egypt. The Israelites were an incredibly stubborn, ungrateful and rebellious people. Moses had chosen to endure and intercede for them for forty years. Despite their repeated failures, Moses neither gave up on them nor wished to see them punished.

Elijah found himself unable to live up to Moses's level of patience. By comparison, Elijah lacked persistence and patience. He gave up when he felt that he was not as great as his predecessors. In fact, Elijah is the only prophet in the Bible who ever appeared before God to accuse the Israelites! Elijah was disappointed that he still faced defeat despite all that he had done. "I can't take it anymore! I'm done!" he exclaimed (my paraphrase).

However, who said that Elijah had to be better than other people? God never said that. It was Elijah's self-imposed standard. God called Moses to be Moses, and He called Elijah to be Elijah. He calls you to be you.

"What are you doing here?"

Let's continue with the story in 1 Kings 19:9-18:

> **9** There he went into a cave and spent the night. And the word of the Lord came to him: "What are you doing here, Elijah?"
>
> **10** He replied, "I have been very zealous for the Lord God Almighty. The Israelites have rejected your covenant, torn down your altars, and put your prophets to death with the sword. I am the only one left, and now they are trying to kill me too."
>
> **11** The Lord said, "Go out and stand on the mountain in the presence of the Lord, for the Lord is about to pass by."
>
> Then a great and powerful wind tore the mountains apart and shattered the rocks before the Lord, but the Lord was not in the wind. After the wind there was an earthquake, but the Lord was not in the earthquake. **12** After the earthquake came a fire, but the Lord was not in the fire. And after the fire came a gentle whisper.
>
> **13** When Elijah heard it, he pulled his cloak over his face and went out and stood at the mouth of the cave. Then a voice said to him, "What are you doing here, Elijah?"
>
> **14** He replied, "I have been very zealous for the Lord God Almighty. The Israelites have rejected your covenant, torn down your altars, and put your prophets to death with the sword. I am the only one left, and now they are trying to kill me too."
>
> **15** The Lord said to him, "Go back the way you came, and go to the Desert of Damascus. When you get there, anoint Hazael king over Aram. **16** Also, anoint Jehu son of Nimshi king over Israel, and anoint Elisha son of Shaphat from Abel Meholah to succeed you as prophet. **17** Jehu will put to death any who escape the sword of Hazael, and Elisha will put to death any who escape the sword of Jehu.

> **18** Yet I reserve seven thousand in Israel—all whose knees have
> not bowed down to Baal and whose mouths have not kissed him."

To understand how God delivered Elijah from the bottom of his pit, we can begin by looking at a recurring pattern in the narrative. 1 Kings 19:9–18 has a symmetrical structure: the Lord questioned Elijah twice, asking "What are you doing here?" and Elijah responded to God twice. After each of Elijah's answers, God instructed him to take action. The first instruction was to come out and stand on the mountain, where strong winds, earthquakes, and fire appeared, but God was not found in any of them. The second time, God directed Elijah to anoint three individuals.

Look first at the question God asked Elijah. The questions God asks are very important, especially when He asks them more than once. When we feel exhausted physically and mentally, we have no awareness of where we're going. Let God ask us: "What are you doing here?"

The verb 'do' is not actually in the original text, and the focus is not on "doing" but on "here". The question God asked was: "Why are you in this current state?"

By asking Elijah in this manner, God prompted him to reflect and identify what had led to his predicament. This approach proved more effective than reprimanding or punishing him. Elijah responded to God's inquiry twice with identical answers, exposing his preconceived beliefs about God and himself.

Elijah said twice:

> "I have been very zealous for the Lord God Almighty. The Israelites
> have rejected your covenant, torn down your altars, and put your
> prophets to death with the sword. I am the only one left, and now
> they are trying to kill me too." (1 Kings 19:10, 14)

Elijah's use of the word 'zealous' indicated his genuine desire to guide the people back to the right path and to focus on worshipping God, something which he considered to be his calling. However, he didn't expect that the outcome would be the opposite of what he desired. He didn't expect that he would end up being chased and in danger of being killed. He might have thought, "I have been so zealous and done so much for the Lord, but it has all been for nothing!"

It is difficult to precisely determine the root of Elijah's complaints based on his words alone; but God's responses to him suggest that Elijah's biggest pain was neither bitterness nor shame, but more likely disappointment: disappointment in his own people, in himself, and perhaps even in God.

Throughout his life, Elijah had dedicated all his time and effort to leading his people away from idol worship and back to the worship of the one true God. Despite the great risks he had taken, including his spectacular victory on Mount Carmel, his efforts had been in vain. Jezebel, the queen, continued to hold sway, and God's people continued to disobey. Elijah came to the shocking realisation that his zealous work had made no difference at all. This realisation was all the more devastating as it came at a time when Elijah was at the end of his rope and could no longer bear the burden.

"I am the only one left!"

Elijah complained to God, "I am the only one left" as if God was unaware of what was actually happening.

The irony in his complaint is hard to ignore. God was addressing Elijah's state of disarray, which mirrored the situation of the hundred prophets hid and fed by Obadiah in a cave when Jezebel killed the prophets of the Lord (1 Kings 18). Elijah should have been aware of the existence of these prophets (see 1 Kings 18:13), yet he lamented to God that he was the only one left, as if these prophets had never been there.

Perhaps he had forgotten them. Perhaps he didn't consider them important because they didn't stand up bravely with him and fight against Baal. Ironically, Elijah was now in the same position as these prophets, hiding in a cave and relying on angels for sustenance. His aspiration of changing his nation and turning people back to God was gone. Elijah had discovered that he was just as helpless as everyone else.

When we believe we're "the only one left", it is often a feeling rather than a fact.

God doesn't have to be in the wind, the earthquake or the fire

How did God help Elijah and respond to his complaints?

First, God commanded Elijah to leave the cave and stand before Him, for He would pass by. A mighty wind immediately blew, followed by an earthquake and a fierce fire, but God was not in any of those phenomena.

In those days, people believed that Baal was the deity responsible for controlling storms, and they hoped that their prayers would bring much-needed rain for their crops. They therefore crafted idols of Baal such that the idols appeared to be summoning wind and rain, similar to what Elijah experienced on Mount Horeb. What they ended up seeing Elijah doing during the confrontation on Mount Carmel – calling fire down onto the sacrifice – was a display of God's magnificent power over an idol believed to be capable of impressive actions which in fact it could not perform.

The truth was that Baal was merely a man-made god, moulded into any form that would fit the popular beliefs, needs and desires of the people who worshipped it. God made it clear that He was different from Baal in every way. He didn't (and doesn't) conform to people's imaginations or follow human commands.

Elijah probably thought that God's presence on Mount Horeb should be as spectacular as on Mount Carmel when God sent down fire from heaven. He believed that God's actions should also be grandiose and impressive, but God was now teaching him: "I may not work in your way. I can work in other ways, perhaps even with just my silence, and not necessarily in the place and time you expect."

God wanted to teach Elijah this lesson: "I may not be what you expect."

The 'silent' voice of God

In 1 Kings 19:12, the passage highlights that there was "a still small voice" (KJV) or a "gentle whisper" (NIV). We find a wide range of translations of this verse because the original text is very difficult to grasp and translate accurately. The literal translation is something like this: 'a sound - silence - breaking (or weakening)'. 'Silence' describes the sound and 'breaking (or weakening)' describes the silence. Perhaps we can put it this way: a sound was heard, but the sound was a broken silence.

Silence and sound are opposites, yet Scripture uses 'silence' to describe this sound, which seems inexplicable. What is the point of this statement? Where was God in this sound when He was not in the wind, earthquake or fire? And how did God help Elijah regain his strength by taking him through this strange experience?

The passage is not saying that God spoke at a very low volume so Elijah had to quiet down to listen. Instead, God was teaching Elijah to let go of his previous expectations and understand that God does not necessarily reveal Himself in a grandiose way. God does not need to speak at all. His presence can be completely silent and still. Let us not misunderstand the focus of the Scripture, thinking that it emphasises stillness. In fact, there is no mention of a still small voice here, and 'broken' does not describe a sound but rather silence.

Immediately, God instructs Elijah to anoint three individuals. Elijah probably thought he had completed his mission on Mount Carmel, overcoming all odds, but that was not the case. He still had work to do, except he was no longer the protagonist of the story. God was calling Elijah to pass the baton to someone else.

The call to let go

The three men whom God wanted Elijah to anoint were significant, but rather unexpected. The king of Aram was Israel's enemy who didn't believe in God, but whom God still used to punish the Israelites, hoping that they would repent. Jehu was also not a righteous person, but God made him the king of Israel to replace Ahab's dynasty. Elisha would take Elijah's place as a prophet.

Interestingly, in the end, Elijah could only anoint one of the three men: Elisha. The other two were anointed by Elisha. Ahab later sincerely repented, so God postponed the punishment of the house of Ahab until after Ahab's death (1 Kings 21:27–29). Therefore, the king of Aram and Jehu appeared later. This was God's plan. He postpones judgment because He desires to see people repent. From this perspective, Elijah's role appeared to be rather insignificant. He could not even fulfil the simple task of anointing three people. In fact, he was only doing the preparatory work because God took him away after he anointed Elisha.

Furthermore, like Elijah, all these three men also eventually failed to eradicate the corrupt Baal worship. This spiritual cancer would persist for a considerable time. The Israelites would continue to worship Baal until they were eventually captured and exiled, indicating that Elijah's aspiration for a single decisive victory would remain unfulfilled.

The lesson for Elijah to learn was an important one. Yes, he performed a great miracle on Mount Carmel for God. Yes, he proved to his people that Baal was a false god. However, Elijah fell into the same pattern of thinking found in Baal worshippers who only saw God according to their own imagination. Elijah's depression may have been rooted in unnecessary stress and disappointment in himself. He thought God had to use him to change the nation of Israel. These false expectations became his drives, blinding him to God's reality. He could see God in the grandiose climax but not in the silent anticlimax.

Even in silence, God is still always present and at work. While Elijah was too busy focusing on himself and his circumstances, God had already prepared a hundred other prophets and seven thousand people still standing in faith, as well as Elisha to carry his baton to the next phase of God's plan. Elijah had to let go of his ego and accept that he was not irreplaceable. Only God can truly change the world, and He may also use other people and means to accomplish His plans.

Letting go is no easy matter

Elijah's self-imposed pressures eventually led him to exhaustion and despair. He lost sight of himself in the process, which is a common pathway to burnout. Burnout can stem from various causes, but misplaced desires and expectations are often the culprits. Elijah felt personally responsible for saving the whole nation by making people repent and turn back to God, convinced that the success of endeavour rested solely on his shoulders. In this process, he transformed what was originally a wonderful desire into a harmful burden by weighing himself down with unnecessary expectations and responsibilities.

If Elijah hadn't held onto these presuppositions, he would have enjoyed his ministry more and spared himself considerable pain. The root of burnout is not in the calling but in a distorted expectation or a distorted self. Whenever we're serving God zealously, we should always ask ourselves, "Is this for me?" There are things in life that we think we ought to do or that we want to do, but they are not essential. Meanwhile, things that *must* be done don't necessarily have to be done by *us*. And if we *must* do them, we may not be responsible for completing every part of the process or completing them *immediately*.

I like to use chess as an analogy. Playing chess requires a game plan. God is the one who sets up the plan and we are His pieces. In a chess game, some pawns may not move at all, but they are often very important. In contrast, the rook can move in any direction quickly and seems powerful, but the chess master doesn't need to use it in most of the moves. Sometimes a knight makes an impressive attack, but sometimes it stands still just to protect a pawn. We are the chess pieces, and each person's position is different at different times. God has a master plan, and His moves may not follow our expectations. God may also set up multiple different plans and have different ways of doing things at different times.

Letting go is not an easy thing to do. I have seen many meddling retirees who constantly impose their ideas on others in work they are no longer responsible for. This situation certainly also exists within the church. The more successful the ministers have been, the harder it is for them to let go and delegate to others or train others to do their job, which results in damage to many ministries. Fortunately, Elijah eventually realised this and was willing to let go and not continue to take everything upon himself.

This is the role that God wanted Elijah to play. It was a role that couldn't be negotiated or fully comprehended by Elijah. Today, if God orders you to play a certain role, it is essential to recognise that you may not see the final results or understand the reason behind it. Be faithful in playing your role and leave the rest to God. Do not impose your expectations on how God should use you. In Elijah's life, the immediate results and accomplishments were not the most important. He had to learn to accept the role God had called him to play and refrain from adding anything else to it. He was only responsible for the tasks God had entrusted him, and when the time came, he needed to pass the baton and let others take over. The race belongs to God.

4

The lost son

The parable of the lost son – traditionally known as the parable of the prodigal son – found in Luke 15:11–32, is one of the most well-known and beloved stories in the Bible. However, most readers often overlook the fact that the story was not originally told by Jesus as a stand-alone story. It is preceded by two parables with a similar theme: the lost sheep and the lost coin (Luke 15:1–10). Gospel authors often use comparisons and contrasts to help readers gain a deeper understanding of the kingdom of God. So, these two shorter parables are there to set the stage for the prodigal son story by giving us important hints on how to understand it.

In other words, readers studying the parable of the prodigal son as a part of a trio may uncover meanings that may not be readily apparent when the parable is read individually. Let us take a closer look at the similarities and differences between the three parables. The main lesson that Jesus is trying to teach us may be a surprising one!

Context is everything

The beginning of Luke's account explains the reason why Jesus told these parables. In 15:1–2, we read,

¹ Now the tax collectors and sinners were all gathering round to hear Jesus. ² But the Pharisees and the teachers of the law muttered, "This man welcomes sinners and eats with them."

The Pharisees believed that Jesus's acceptance of tax collectors and sinners was wrong, so Jesus used the three parables to address their thinking. We need to read the story of the prodigal son in this context: it is a response to the Pharisees' perspectives on sinners.

Parables often have two meanings, one on the surface and one deeper. The surface meaning is usually easy to understand, such as the Prodigal Son returning and his father accepting him. However, parables also have a much deeper level of understanding. First, let's look at the parables of the lost sheep and the lost coin:

³ Then Jesus told them this parable: ⁴ "Suppose one of you has a hundred sheep and loses one of them. Doesn't he leave the ninety-nine in the open country and go after the lost sheep until he finds it? ⁵ And when he finds it, he joyfully puts it on his shoulders ⁶ and goes home. Then he calls his friends and neighbours together and says, 'Rejoice with me; I have found my lost sheep.' ⁷ I tell you that in the same way there will be more rejoicing in heaven over one sinner who repents than over ninety-nine righteous persons who do not need to repent. ⁸ "Or suppose a woman has ten silver coins and loses one. Doesn't she light a lamp, sweep the house and search carefully until she finds it? ⁹ And when she finds it, she calls her friends and neighbours together and says, 'Rejoice with me; I have found my lost coin.' ¹⁰ In the same way, I tell you, there is rejoicing in the presence of the angels of God over one sinner who repents." (Luke 15:3–10)

Comparing the three parables of loss

Let us first look at the first two shorter parables (the lost sheep and the lost coin). They have many similarities:

1. In both stories, something precious is lost and is actively sought after by the owner.
2. Both lost items are just a small part of the whole, but the owners still search very hard: one leaves 99 sheep to find one lost sheep while the other searches every corner of the house to find a lost coin.
3. Both owners find what was lost, and both are so overjoyed that they invite others to celebrate with them.
4. Finally, Jesus emphasises that there will be rejoicing in heaven over one sinner who repents.

The lesson from the two parables is clear: it is absolutely worth rejoicing over one sinner's repentance. This was clearly aimed at the Pharisees, who always looked down on people they perceived as 'sinners'. Seeing Jesus accept sinners frustrated them; Jesus had to show them how God's perspectives are different from theirs. Luke's account guides readers to understand these two parables in this direction.

But what about the lost son? Let's look at the text in verses 11–32:

> [11] Jesus continued: "There was a man who had two sons. [12] The younger one said to his father, 'Father, give me my share of the estate.' So he divided his property between them. [13] Not long after that, the younger son got together all he had, set off for a distant country and there squandered his wealth in wild living.
>
> [14] After he had spent everything, there was a severe famine in that whole country, and he began to be in need. [15] So he went and hired himself out to a citizen of that country, who sent him to his fields to feed pigs. [16] He longed to fill his stomach with the pods

that the pigs were eating, but no one gave him anything.

¹⁷ "When he came to his senses, he said, 'How many of my father's hired servants have food to spare, and here I am starving to death! ¹⁸ I will set out and go back to my father and say to him: Father, I have sinned against heaven and against you. ¹⁹ I am no longer worthy to be called your son; make me like one of your hired servants.'

²⁰ So he got up and went to his father. But while he was still a long way off, his father saw him and was filled with compassion for him; he ran to his son, threw his arms round him and kissed him.

²¹ "The son said to him, 'Father, I have sinned against heaven and against you. I am no longer worthy to be called your son.'

²² "But the father said to his servants, 'Quick! Bring the best robe and put it on him. Put a ring on his finger and sandals on his feet. ²³ Bring the fattened calf and kill it. Let's have a feast and celebrate. ²⁴ For this son of mine was dead and is alive again; he was lost and is found.' So they began to celebrate.

²⁵ "Meanwhile, the elder son was in the field. When he came near the house, he heard music and dancing. ²⁶ So he called one of the servants and asked him what was going on. ²⁷ 'Your brother has come,' he replied, 'and your father has killed the fattened calf because he has him back safe and sound.'

²⁸ "The elder brother became angry and refused to go in. So his father went out and pleaded with him. ²⁹ But he answered his father, 'Look! All these years I've been slaving for you and never disobeyed your orders. Yet you never gave me even a young goat so I could celebrate with my friends. ³⁰ But when this son of yours who has squandered your property with prostitutes comes home, you kill the fattened calf for him!'

³¹ "'My son,' the father said, 'you are always with me, and everything I have is yours. ³² But we had to celebrate and be glad,

> because this brother of yours was dead and is alive again; he was
> lost and is found.'"

How is the prodigal son story similar to the two preludes? First, the father is also overjoyed and wants to throw a big celebration, just like the owners of the sheep and the coin. Second, the father also stresses that what was lost has been found.

However, apart from these two similarities, there are several startling differences.

One shocking difference is that the father doesn't actively go out to search for his son. He doesn't even seem bothered at all at first. He simply allows the son to get 'lost' and then just passively waits at home for him to return. This clearly doesn't match the previous two parables. Why did Jesus tell the story this way? The previous parables suggest the owners desperately search everywhere for what is lost. This would have made the story more touching and dramatic, but this is not the story Jesus told in the third parable.

Another striking difference is in the celebration. In the first two parables, everyone is celebrating joyfully. But in the parable of the prodigal son, someone is upset to the point of refusing to be part of the celebration. Notice how the older brother's argument with the father takes up a substantial proportion of the story. His reaction poses a striking contrast to the father's, as well as with the people mentioned in the previous parables.

Finally, there is a puzzling difference between the details highlighted in the stories. The first two parables don't explain how the sheep and the coin become lost in the beginning. They seem to have suddenly become lost one day. Yet both parables describe the details of the search campaigns and the amount of effort being put into them. The story of the prodigal son, however, is the exact opposite. It gives a detailed account of the process by which the son becomes lost, but there is no mention of the father going out to search for him.

Couldn't the story be told in a more touching and consistent way? We would probably picture the story like this: the pitiful son has decided to never come back home, so the father leaves everything behind and desperately travels to distant lands to search for him. And when the father finally finds him, he and the older son both rejoice. Then the family lives happily ever after.

Wouldn't this version be more powerful, more gospel-like, and more in line with the previous two parables? This storyline would have been more logical if Jesus had only wanted to highlight how the loving father perseveres in searching for his son. Why didn't Jesus tell the story this way? His version is a bit unexpected. Let us look closer at the details.

At which moment does the son become a lost son?

The disparities between the prodigal son story and the previous two parables reveal the true message Jesus intended to convey. The answers can be found in the details Jesus included in the story. There are two kinds of useful hints we can use while understanding narratives in Scripture. First, the lengths of the different sections of the text can reflect where the focus of the passage lies. Second, repetition is usually an important indicator of significance, especially when the author chooses to use direct speech.

Therefore, if Jesus meticulously elaborated on a certain part of the story, if he used direct speech, and then repeated that same speech, we know we need to pay extra attention. This is exactly what we find in this story. The younger son's speech to his father after he returns home is given in direct speech, and is repeated twice:

> "Father, I have sinned against heaven and against you. I am no longer worthy to be called your son." (vv. 18–19, 21)

The younger son is fully aware of the magnitude of his wrongdoing, and he feels too ashamed to face his father. On the surface, what the son is saying appears to be out of humility because he is admitting his mistakes and making an effort to change. But in reality, it is a kind of pride. His intention is not to restore his relationship with his father but to become a mere worker. This way, he can avoid facing his shameful actions as a son.

He intends to continue with his planned speech: "Make me like one of your hired servants" (v. 19). He is simply trying to make a deal so he can have a better life. By becoming a hired worker, all he needs to do is become one of the servants and provide for himself, without facing his father as his father. He can rely on his own efforts and feel better about himself.

This is when the father interrupts abruptly. The moment the father stops his son's speech is the key to our understanding of what Jesus is trying to teach us. The father didn't stop his son from taking his inheritance and spending the money elsewhere, because he was still his son. The son's identity never changed despite his mistakes. This is why the father didn't need to go out to search for him. But the moment the son shows unwillingness to approach the father as a son and attempts instead to become a hired worker, the father must stop him immediately, or else this is the moment the son becomes lost because the precious father-son relationship is gone.

There is only one way to return home: as a beloved son

The father hasn't lost an employee. He lost a son, not because the son left home or wasted his money, but because he no longer sees himself as the son. The father must reclaim this lost relationship at all costs. How does he do it? He immediately halts his son's speech and commands the servants to quickly bring and put on the son a robe, shoes, and a ring, restoring him to his rightful position as a son. The father forbids the son from becoming a hired worker. It is absolutely unacceptable to the father to lose this relationship.

Both the robe and the ring are unmistakable status symbols of sonship. Workers are never given either of these. They represent a status almost equal to that of the father. The ring has an additional meaning: in ancient times, the family seal was often engraved on the family ring. People could withdraw money with the ring seal, like a modern-day credit card. The text points out that the father has to prohibit his son from being a hired worker. All he cares about is the son's true identity, and he needs to let his son know very clearly, "You are not a worker; you are my son!"

Some people may consider this father's actions unwise. He is spoiling an unruly child. Surely no sensible father would reward a son who has just ruined the family's inheritance so badly by showering him with lavish gifts. Yet Jesus's teaching is not about parenting techniques but about who we really are when we approach God. Approaching God is returning home. As far as God is concerned, there is only one way for us to return home – as sons or daughters. Yet in this story, the son thinks he's going for a job interview rather than going home. How tragic! If we think we have to earn our way back to God, we have not understood the gospel at all.

Only when the son comes home as the son can he re-embrace his original relationship with the father. This is the relationship he has always had since birth. A son's identity comes from birth with no conditions attached. It is the most precious thing he possesses. And it is as simple as that. Likewise, it is only when we truly know who we are in God can we truly come home. Who are we? We are the children of God who are loved unconditionally by our Father. Often, we tend to make our relationship with God complicated because we can't fully grasp how unconditional the Father's love is for us.

Imagine if the father in the parable had accepted his son as a hired worker just as he had requested. Would the son be able to make amends for his past mistakes by being a worker? No! He might make a living, but he can never truly return home unless the father chooses to accept him as his son. There is nothing he can do to earn the relationship back. The son says he is not worthy to be the son. But it is not the son's decision to decide whether he's worthy to return home or not. It is the father's decision. The good news is that the father is resolved to welcome the son as his beloved son.

Like the younger son, we have made irreparable mistakes in our lives. I once watched the testimony of a murderer who had accepted Christ in prison. None of his family and friends accepted him or wanted to have anything to do with him. He didn't blame them, because even he couldn't accept himself. Truly, only our Father in heaven can forgive sinners. He has made it clear He will not annul our status as sons and daughters; He can't tolerate even having us as mere hired workers. He must welcome us back as His sons and daughters. Such is God's stubborn, unconditional love.

The older brother: the other Prodigal Son

Next, let's look at the elder son. Verses 25 to 32 detail the reaction of the older son when he learns about the big party the father is going to throw to celebrate the return of his brother. His reaction is probably how most people would have responded in the same situation.

If you understand the essence of what Jesus is trying to teach here, you will realise there are two prodigal sons in the story. Both sons are equally lost because they both never see themselves as sons but merely as hired workers. Both focus on calculating how much work they need to do to earn enough merit to be their father's sons. Although the eldest son appears to be staying at home with the father the whole time, he has failed to understand the relationship that the father desires, just like his brother.

The Pharisees resemble the elder son, thinking that they must do something to please God. They focus on people's mistakes and merits rather than their identity in God's eyes. Even when someone repents, they still believe that they must accumulate enough merits necessary for them to enter God's kingdom. They take pride in their accomplishments and look down on others as less worthy.

Many Christians who serve God faithfully understand it's wrong to judge other people negatively, but they still unconsciously judge themselves and regard themselves as hired labour, working very hard to earn God's favour. This is something I keep reminding my students at the theological seminary where I teach. We must examine our lives and ministries from the perspective of our true identity as God's children. A seminary alumnus who graduated ten years ago came to see me one day. He said he had heard me give a sermon on Christian sonship ten years ago, and he didn't understand why I chose to emphasise this particular topic. But after serving God for ten years, he finally realised how important this was. Why? This awakening is the true and only source of motivation for ministry.

Sometimes, our motivation comes from the desire to do more and be better, not from seeing who we are and how we are in God's eyes. We find it incredibly difficult to accept free grace and unconditional acceptance. We seem to feel more comfortable if there is a clear list of conditions for us to follow. The Bible, however, has made it clear that salvation is 100% by grace. This doesn't mean we don't need to do anything or give up anything to be Christians. We are called to carry our cross to follow Jesus, but we can't rely on what we do for our salvation. This is what is so unique about Christianity. Not only does God's acceptance not come with conditions, but it would also be impossible for us to meet the conditions if they existed. Who you are, not how you work, is what matters. You are not becoming God's child; you *are* God's child.

Have you truly returned home to your Father?

The parable never discloses how both sons react to the father's display of love. Do they understand their father's heart in the end? We don't know. We're all on the same learning curve as these two sons about the profound significance of coming home. The question then arises: what do we have to do to come home to the Father? Nothing! This is the answer that lies at the heart of the matter. True homecoming lies solely in the Father's unconditional acceptance, where our inherent worth surpasses any achievements or shortcomings. It is a reminder that our place in this home is not earned by any duty or transaction but simply by our original divine heritage as sons and daughters of God.

In contemplating this story, we are reminded of the life of Jesus, who, as the Son, willingly took up the role of a servant. He "humbled himself by becoming obedient to death – even death on a cross" (Philippians 2:8). Before commencing his ministry, when Jesus received baptism, the Heavenly Father declared, "This is my Son, whom I love" (Matthew 3:17). God first affirmed Jesus's identity as the beloved Son before his ministry began. Our capacity to truly give and sacrifice stems from embracing the assurance inherent in our bestowed identity.

May we learn to understand the essence of homecoming as the embrace of a loving Father, without conditions or strings attached. And may we, inspired by the sacrificial love of Jesus, find the courage to give and sacrifice, rooted in the firm foundation of our divine identity.

III

Who are you in God?

A distorted self resulting in a distorted relationship

5

The wicked servant

In the previous section, we saw how a distorted sense of self tragically distorts a person's perceptions of his life circumstances as well as God's calling. This section further examines how a distorted sense of calling leads to a distorted relationship with God. We will start with one of the most intriguing parables Jesus told: the parable of the three servants who are entrusted with different amounts of wealth (talents) by their master (Matthew 25:14–30). It is intriguing because it offers profound insights into the consequences of a distorted sense of calling.

Before dissecting this parable, it's essential to emphasise the significance of understanding its context, as discussed earlier. The parable of the talents is immediately preceded by another parable called the parable of the ten virgins. In this parable, five wise virgins are well-prepared for their master's return. The other five, in contrast, indulged in idleness during the master's absence. They are unprepared and caught off guard when the master arrives, with disastrous consequences. This theme of preparedness gives us a hint of how to read the parable of the talents (called the parable of the bags of gold in newer translations).

While the preceding parable deals with the issue of making preparation to meet God, the parable of the talents deals with the question of what it means to be prepared. God has given each one of us all kinds of resources including relationships, opportunities and capabilities. The possibilities of what we can do with them are unlimited. The heart of the matter is whether we're ready to utilise what God has entrusted us with.

Let's first look at Matthew 25:14–19 (ESV):

> 14 "For it will be like a man going on a journey, who called his servants and entrusted to them his property. 15 To one he gave five talents, to another two, to another one, to each according to his ability. Then he went away. 16 He who had received the five talents went at once and traded with them, and he made five talents more. 17 So also he who had the two talents made two talents more. 18 But he who had received the one talent went and dug in the ground and hid his master's money. 19 Now after a long time the master of those servants came and settled accounts with them."

A type of trust that doesn't come with clear instructions

The passage describes three servants entrusted with responsibilities by their master, followed by the outcomes of their respective endeavours. The three servants share some similarities and differences.

Let's look at the obvious similarities first. None of them receives explicit instructions regarding what to do with the talents. The passage doesn't mention anything about what the master expects them to do with the resources. The story seems to imply that the master assumes they know.

This lack of instructions is particularly shocking and frustrating to many Christians I know. They expect the Christian life to be about waiting for God to tell them exactly what major they should study at university, which job to choose, who to marry, which house to rent, etc. Sometimes, praying for guidance is reduced to a form of fortune-telling. Somehow, they feel more 'holy' if they keep waiting for God to make decisions for them. And they feel lost when the specific instructions they have been earnestly praying for never come.

In the story, all the responsibility and the decision-making regarding what to do with the resources lies in the servants' hands. This makes perfect sense. When the master is away, the best person to make the right decision for the resources is someone who has the resources. It wouldn't be wise if the master tried to control exactly what the servants should do. A relationship built on mutual trust doesn't always need an instructional manual.

The second similarity is that although the amount of talents of the three servants varies significantly, they are treated equally because the master distributes the talents "to each according to his ability" (v. 15). Again, this is not unusual at all. If you have ever been an employer or a boss, you will understand very well the important principle of knowing your people's abilities and entrusting resources to them accordingly. God grants each of us ample room to exercise His gifts, regardless of whether the gifts are the same or our abilities are equivalent.

Two different magnitudes of achievements, identical praise

Furthermore, the servant who receives five talents and the one who receives two talents also share a couple of similarities. Let's consider verses 20–23:

> [20] "And he who had received the five talents came forward, bringing five talents more, saying, 'Master, you delivered to me five talents; here, I have made five talents more.' [21] His master said to him, 'Well done, good and faithful servant. You have been faithful over a little; I will set you over much. Enter into the joy of your master.' [22] And he also who had the two talents came forward, saying, 'Master, you delivered to me two talents; here, I have made two talents more.' [23] His master said to him, 'Well done, good and faithful servant. You have been faithful over a little; I will set you over much. Enter into the joy of your master.'"

Both servants engage in business and double their wealth. We're probably very curious to know how on earth they manage to achieve such a high yield.

But it's clear Jesus didn't think it was important enough to be mentioned. This is not the point of the story.

The point of the story can be found in what Jesus chose to repeat and highlight. When it is time to settle accounts, they joyfully present their achievements to the master in the same way:

> 'Master,' he said, 'you delivered to me five/two talents. See, I have made five/two talents more.' (vv. 20 and 22)

This quote clearly reveals how they view their relationship with the master. The master is the provider of resources and gifts, which they see as great opportunities for them to utilise and multiply. Finally, they happily celebrate the results with the master.

The second similarity between the first two servants is the master's praise for them:

> His master replied, "Well done, good and faithful servant. You have been faithful over a little; I will set you over much. Enter into the joy of your master." (vv. 21 and 23)

Although the difference in the amount of wealth earned by the two servants is great, the praise they receive from the master is identical. The author deliberately repeats the master's quotes identically, illustrating that God is not concerned with our achievements but rather with our faithfulness.

What's so wicked about the wicked servant?

The third servant, however, is different. He doesn't invest the money in anything. He doesn't earn a single cent and returns the same money straight to the master while complaining about him. Let's explore verses 24–27:

24 "He also who had received the one talent came forward, saying, 'Master, I knew you to be a hard man, reaping where you did not sow, and gathering where you scattered no seed, 25 so I was afraid, and I went and hid your talent in the ground. Here, you have what is yours.' 26 But his master answered him, 'You wicked and slothful servant! You knew that I reap where I have not sown and gather where I scattered no seed? 27 Then you ought to have invested my money with the bankers, and at my coming I should have received what was my own with interest.'"

I'd like to point out that burying coins under the ground was a very common practice at the time. It was one of the safest ways to protect wealth in ancient times. It guaranteed the coins wouldn't be lost, but it also meant they wouldn't be put to good use.

And why does the master rebuke him as "wicked and slothful"? The slothful part is understandable because he has hardly done anything. But why is he "wicked"? Perhaps he is just a bit reserved and not a big risk-taker in investments. That shouldn't make him wicked, right? He's merely not as aggressive as the other two in investing. Furthermore, the master never instructed him on what to do, so it can't be entirely his fault. Why condemn him as wicked?

Let's analyse the issues with the third servant and his perception of the master. He hasn't done anything, but ironically, he has said a lot of things! He begins his speech by describing his master:

'I knew you to be a hard man, reaping where you did not sow, and gathering where you scattered no seed' (v. 24).

He is basically complaining that the master is unfair and his expectations are unreasonable. This is a negative way to approach a superior, with clear hints of bitterness and resentment.

Some believers fall into a similar pattern of thoughts. They like to compare their lives to someone else's life, either measuring themselves against those less fortunate than they to feel better, or to those more blessed than they to conclude that God treats them unfairly. Sometimes we allow these unhealthy comparisons to distort our true selves. Our vision becomes obscured, and we start perceiving God as particularly unfair, unkind, and ungracious toward us. A Christian once said, "I'm not sharing the gospel because God hasn't made me Billy Graham." Some of us find ourselves mentally trapped by past failures or regrets, allowing them to hinder us and discourage us. These are all things we must be cautious of in our pursuit of our true selves.

The servant goes on to give an excuse: "I was afraid" (v. 25).

What was he possibly afraid of? The other two servants would logically have more reasons to be afraid as they took far greater risks and responsibilities. But they show no signs of fear, only immense joy. Is the third servant afraid of looking bad when compared to the other two servants? We don't know. But have we ever been afraid of putting what God has entrusted us into good use? What is your fear? The first two servants experience a beautiful partnership with their master, developing full mutual trust. The third servant, however, has no trust in his master. No relationship can thrive when one side doubts the goodness of the other side.

In fact, not trusting God's goodness is one of the major roots of sin. Genesis 3 recounts the story of humanity's first downfall. When the serpent, the devil, tried to deceive and tempt Eve to sin, it began by exploiting this fear that is rooted in doubt. This lies at the core of our fundamental problem. The serpent didn't say, "Look, this fruit is delicious!" Rather, it sowed the seeds of doubt about God's goodness, aiming to undermine Eve's trust in God and make her believe that God had unkind intentions. Essentially, it insinuated, "Do you believe God is good to you? If you think so, you're being naive! He doesn't want you to eat the fruit because He's afraid your eyes will be opened, just like His." The serpent subtly planted the thought that "God is not so good" in Eve's mind. Sowing doubt in God's love for us is the most dangerous and cunning trap.

You can never entrust something important to someone who doesn't trust that you are good. Therefore, this parable of the talent not only addresses the issue of faithfulness but also focuses on how the wicked servant perceives himself in relation to the master and the resources entrusted to him. Comparing the words of this servant to those of the other two, we notice a significant difference. The ones entrusted with five and two talents recognise it is the master's action of giving that has empowered them to achieve their success. In contrast, the third servant says, "I was afraid, and I went and hid your talent in the ground. Here, you have what is yours." (v. 25).

The latter never sees that there's a meaningful partnership, let alone empowerment. What he's implying is, "This is your money. Look, I haven't touched it because it's none of my business. Take it away. I refuse to have anything to do with it." It's akin to going on strike. He is rejecting any partnership role with the master in his business.

The wickedness is found in his rejection of the relationship and his attempt to shift the blame onto the master instead of taking responsibility. This is rebellion because he should recognise that what he's doing is against the master's will. The disobedience arises from his distorted understanding of his relationship with the master. Just like the prodigal son who fails to appreciate the valuable father-son bond and the inheritance he always had, this third servant fails to grasp the valuable partnership and opportunities the master wants to share with him. His lack of trust prevents him from recognising the master's generosity in entrusting him with one talent. It is contrary to the master's will.

The waste of one talent

Compared to the five and two talents, the one talent may not sound like a lot of money, but it was still a huge sum at the time. Some estimates suggest that a talent in Jesus's time would be worth a million US dollars today. Another suggests that a talent represented a person's weight in gold. That's a lot of gold! To put it in perspective, we can compare it with the 30 pieces of silver Judas got for handing Jesus over to the religious authorities (less than 0.1% of a talent)! Even the one talent the master entrusts to the third servant has huge potential for investment possibilities and exciting endeavours.

The parable emphasises that the master gives according to abilities, but he settles the accounts according to faithfulness. There are individuals among us who face significant limitations in terms of resources and opportunities in life. God doesn't look at the results of their work but their faithfulness in living out each day. I have encountered Christians who are bravely fighting terminal illnesses, knowing they have only a short time left to live. Despite their lives being cut short, they exemplify remarkable faithfulness and make the most of the limited opportunities they have to honour and glorify God during their remaining time on earth. This is what our Master in heaven wants.

Some people may feel inclined to defend this servant, arguing that he is not as bad as those who gamble or waste money, like the prodigal son. At least this servant didn't lose any of the capital. However, even if he had suffered losses, the master wouldn't have blamed him because he had to entrust the management of his property to his servants while he was away. Investments always involve risks. If there had been an economic recession at that time, all three servants would have been in equally big trouble. Being reserved in investments is not an excuse. Moreover, as the master suggests, the servant has had the opportunity to earn some interest on the money. Ultimately, the servant bears full responsibility for the failure to generate returns.

Embracing what God has entrusted to us is embracing our calling

Our Master has entrusted each one of us with very different gifts and resources on earth. These don't always come with specific instructions. The more we know our Master, the more we know His heart and what pleases Him. The challenge may be very different from our expectations. But we can trust that the Master knows what He's doing when He gives us these things. If we allow our conflicting expectations to be the excuse to bury our talents, we are essentially burying God's calling for us and miss out on the great opportunity and partnership the Master desires to share with us.

Jesus ended the parable with some harsh words:

[29] "For to everyone who has will more be given, and he will have an abundance. But from the one who has not, even what he has will be taken away. [30] And cast the worthless servant into the outer darkness. In that place there will be weeping and gnashing of teeth." (Matthew 25:29–30)

There are several ways this statement may be misinterpreted. One misunderstanding is to think we should take away from poor people and give to the rich. This is how the gap between the rich and the poor is widening in our society. This is obviously not what God wants. The second wrong application may happen in workplaces and churches, where individuals who serve faithfully always end up with more responsibilities and duties. The more capable you are, the busier you become. This phenomenon is unfortunately true, but it's not what Jesus is saying here. Another way to misinterpret this statement is to assume that God will reward us with more wealth if we are more ambitious in our work. This isn't what Jesus is saying through this parable either.

Jesus is highlighting a fundamental principle of handling the resources God has entrusted to us. When we put them to good use, God will make us stewards of more. All these are gifts from God. A simple analogy is the muscles in our body. We all have muscles. The more we use and train our muscles, the stronger and more capable they become. The less we exercise, the weaker our muscles will be. They will even shrink in mass.

The same principle can be seen in shoes. Have you ever left a pair of new shoes in a storage cupboard for a long time without wearing them? Soon they degrade by themselves, faster than shoes that are worn every day.

Is the master being harsh to the third servant, then? Not really. The servant never really owns that one talent anyway. The master doesn't owe him anything or take anything away from him. It's the servant himself who has chosen to reject his identity as the rightful steward of the talent. He himself has taken away this wealth of resources and opportunity, as well as the relationship with the master. If the master had never given him that talent, the end result would have been the same as him burying the talent.

Today, God is willing to entrust all sorts of capital and opportunities to us according to our abilities. It's important to remember that both the original capital and the yield are gifts from God. As faithful stewards, we can joyfully receive these gifts and put them to good use. Trusting God's goodness means there's no need to compare, complain, fear or doubt. Our calling is to embrace this exciting partnership and enjoy the process.

6

The rich young man

The ancient world has gifted humanity with the Seven Wonders. These extraordinary structures inspire both awe and a sense of mystery. The Bible also offers us its own collection of wonders, with enigmatic passages that leave us wondering. To me, the story of a young man (traditionally called the rich young ruler) coming before Jesus with a question about eternal life is undoubtedly one of these passages.

In this chapter, we will continue to explore the impact of misconceptions about our relationship with God and how they hinder us from understanding and living out our divine calling. We will examine this well-known conversation between Jesus and the young man. Jesus's response held varying levels of complexity due to the religious context of the time. Nonetheless, the story serves as another powerful testament to the significance of clearly understanding how God relates to and calls each of us.

> ^{17} As Jesus started on his way, a man ran up to him and fell on his knees before him. "Good teacher," he asked, "what must I do to inherit eternal life?"
>
> ^{18} "Why do you call me good?" Jesus answered. "No one is good – except God alone. ^{19} You know the commandments: 'You shall

not murder, you shall not commit adultery, you shall not steal, you shall not give false testimony, you shall not defraud, honour your father and mother.'"

²⁰ "Teacher," he declared, "all these I have kept since I was a boy."

²¹ Jesus looked at him and loved him. "One thing you lack," he said. "Go, sell everything you have and give to the poor, and you will have treasure in heaven. Then come, follow me."

²² At this the man's face fell. He went away sad, because he had great wealth. ²³ Jesus looked round and said to his disciples, "How hard it is for the rich to enter the kingdom of God!"

²⁴ The disciples were amazed at his words. But Jesus said again, "Children, how hard it is to enter the kingdom of God! ²⁵ It is easier for a camel to go through the eye of a needle than for someone who is rich to enter the kingdom of God."

²⁶ The disciples were even more amazed, and said to each other, "Who then can be saved?"

²⁷ Jesus looked at them and said, "With man this is impossible, but not with God; all things are possible with God." (Mark 10:17–27)

Everyone is caught by surprise

At first glance, the story appears deceptively simple. However, understanding its message requires us to dig deeper. The most common interpretation goes something like this: this rich, devout man desired to go to heaven, but he was still attached to his possessions. When Jesus challenged him to give everything to the poor, he found out he couldn't let go of his wealth, so he walked away from Jesus. According to this interpretation, God desires for His people to be willing to give up all their wealth and possessions to the poor.

If this is what Jesus was saying, the subsequent events depicted in the passage would seem rather strange. Jesus proclaimed that it is challenging for the rich to enter the kingdom of heaven, which is understandable since the more wealth one possesses, the harder it is to let go. However, why does the text mention that the disciples "were amazed" at Jesus's words (v. 24)? The rich young man was not the only person caught by surprise here. The disciples were, too. Furthermore, the author deliberately repeats how great their astonishment was, stressing that they were "even more amazed" (v. 26). Also, why does the author focus more on the disciples' shock than the rich young man's shock?

At that time, Jesus's disciples had already left everything to follow him. They should have been delighted to hear Jesus telling a rich man to give all his money to the poor in order to follow him. Why were they so shocked? We find ourselves bewildered by their bewilderment. How do we explain the author's repeated emphasis on the disciples' confusion? And why did the disciples ask Jesus, "Who then can be saved?" (v. 26) Their question implied that this rich young man shouldn't have a problem being accepted by God. That is not what modern readers would expect for someone who refused to give up his wealth for God. There must be more to this passage than meets the eye.

What the rich young man is really asking

To answer these questions, we'll have to start from the beginning. First, let's look at the rich young man's initial question to Jesus:

> "Good Teacher, . . . what must I do to inherit eternal life?" (v. 17).

From the way he approached Jesus and knelt before Him, it is evident that he was very devout. No wonder Jesus took a liking to him. How would we expect Jesus to answer this question? For us, the answer is obvious. If you're from the Protestant evangelical tradition, you'll probably expect Jesus to reply, "You must believe in Me" or "You are saved by faith alone." However, Jesus surprises us by answering, "You know the commandments: 'You shall not murder, you shall not commit adultery, you shall not steal...'" – a perplexing response indeed.

Jesus's answer stemmed from the religious context of that time. One key fact I need to point out is that the "eternal life" mentioned by the rich man differs greatly from the idea of eternal life we talk about today when we say, "Believe in Jesus and you'll have eternal life." In first-century Palestine, Jewish society was very religious and everyone believed in God. Jews believed they were God's only chosen people, so the question the rich man was asking was not about being 'saved', as in going to heaven. If it were, Jesus would have simply told the man to believe in Him. The actual question the rich man was genuinely asking was: "How can I be more righteous?"

Becoming righteous was a primary concern for religious Jews. Their belief derived from the book of Habakkuk, which proclaims, "The righteous person will live by his faithfulness" (Habakkuk 2:4). In their understanding, a "righteous person" referred to someone who pleased God. It is highly likely that the rich man's question emerged from the depths of his heart, asking, "What should I do more in order to please God more?" This question is an appropriate one, and Jesus didn't discourage him from asking.

However, before answering, Jesus threw a question back to him: "Why do you call me good?" (v. 18). Jesus's intention was to examine the definition of goodness – what pleases God. Only God can be considered truly good. It is possible that this man had already sought advice from various teachers and diligently followed their instructions, fearing that he might have missed something.

Nevertheless, Jesus still answered his question: to please God, one must do what God commands, which includes observing a series of commandments. What Jesus said here aligns with the teachings of Judaism and the Old Testament. This is the typical answer Jewish rabbis would give. The rich man claimed to have followed all these commandments, to which Jesus replied, "One thing you lack: Go, sell everything you have and give to the poor, and you will have treasure in heaven. Then come, follow me" (v. 21).

True piety, false piety

Jesus was not implying that the man needed to add one more commandment to his long checklist. Rather, he pointed out that something needed to be subtracted. It was not about doing more but having less.

The author then chooses to focus more on the disciples' reactions than on the rich man's reaction. It became evident that their confusion was not related to the concept of giving up wealth for Jesus, as they all comprehended this aspect quite well. Why, then, were they so perplexed by Jesus's comments?

The best explanation lies in the context of Judaism at the time. This man knew that according to Judaism, he must observe many laws. He had been following all those that he knew about. However, in those days, the Pharisees also added lots of man-made rules and rituals that people had to observe in addition to the Law of Moses in order to be 'more righteous'. These rules included offering more sacrifices during religious festivals, regularly giving to the poor, constructing synagogues and building bridges and roads. In the Pharisees' eyes, a person's spirituality was intricately tied to these activities, all of which required money; observing the Pharisees' man-made obligations was a substantial financial burden. Wealthy people could more easily fulfil these obligations than people of lesser means. Some even hired others to perform acts of kindness on their behalf.

As a result, wealthy individuals were the only ones who could fully comply with all the commandments. Their wealth was the key factor that enabled them to do more 'righteous' things. The poor, on the other hand, were considered 'less righteous' because they simply couldn't afford these extra acts of service. It was widely believed, then, that it was difficult for the poor to enter God's kingdom. This is why Jesus's statement left the disciples dumbfounded. It was the exact opposite of the popular belief at the time.

Once we understand the context, we can interpret the story very differently. First, let's not assume that this rich young man loved money more than God. He might have genuinely been trying hard to be righteous, and he thought he needed the money to do so. He came to Jesus, presenting himself as someone with both wealth and a willing heart. His challenge to Jesus was clear: "Tell me what else I must do. You name any condition you want. No matter what you propose, I can surely do it because I have the wealth."

On the surface, he appeared fully devoted to God, but in reality, it was all pride. Consequently, Jesus set a condition that completely turned his religious worldview upside down: "Sell everything you have . . . give to the poor . . . follow me" (v. 21). Jesus was saying, "Get rid of everything you think will make you more righteous and justified, and instead, completely rely on me." From this perspective, we can understand why "the man's face fell" and why "he went away sad" (v. 22) after hearing Jesus's words.

Relying on God, not on ourselves

Jesus's main point was not that we must sell all our possessions and give to the poor in order to be saved. If this is a prerequisite for salvation, then we are not saved by grace and faith alone. Moreover, this commandment is not found in other teachings of Jesus or in the rest of the Bible. We may breathe a sigh of relief, but what Jesus was demanding is very challenging to many of us.

So, what exactly was Jesus trying to say?

Jesus declared that any means of self-righteousness or things we rely on to be closer to God are inadequate to make us righteous in God's eyes. We must let go of them and rely solely on Jesus. This man decided he could not let go of his wealth because he thought his wealth allowed him to earn more merits and get closer to God.

Judaism finds itself easily falling into this pattern of thinking, where individuals seek to please God through their own means, transforming it into a self-centred, man-made religion. The Pharisees manipulated widows' resources, not necessarily out of greed but to gain more financial power to establish their reputation and boast of their ability to meet God's requirements. The rich man in Mark's Gospel could not let go of his possessions because he depended on them to serve God. It was not greed but reliance on his resources that hindered him. It's all human nature.

This tendency towards self-righteousness can take different forms in different people. Perhaps an experienced worship leader thinks he is more pleasing to God because his songs move people's hearts. Perhaps a church elder thinks he's more spiritual because he has been serving the church diligently even before other church members were born. Perhaps a founder of a Christian charity feels good about himself because his charity has helped thousands of poor people. Perhaps a Christian intellectual thinks he's important in God's kingdom because he's very good at debating with atheists. Now imagine if Jesus told all these individuals to give up these gifts. It wouldn't be easy. How would they see their place in God's kingdom without these things that have defined how they serve God? This is why Jesus's comment was so shocking to the disciples.

Responding to God's calling is not a means to earn God's favour

These individuals may think all these wonderful gifts are their 'calling' from God. They may be. But if the gifts and resources become a way to earn spiritual merit or a reason to feel more important in God's kingdom, they are no longer a calling, but something you must surrender if you want to truly follow Jesus.

We each have our hidden sense of spiritual pride or streaks of self-righteousness that affect how we serve God. What's yours? Is there anything that you have that makes you feel you're more 'spiritual' than others? These things are the most difficult to give up. We don't want to acknowledge our complete helplessness before God and that we have nothing to bring to the table of salvation. The ones who consider themselves most qualified to earn God's favour are the most difficult to save because they are unwilling to let go of their pride. Hence, unless we abandon our self-proclaimed 'righteousness' and rely on Jesus alone, we cannot be saved.

I love to use gliding as an analogy. Gliders have no engines. The point of gliding is *not* to invent the best engine. A glider simply relies on the wind to soar. Even if we create a really good engine, the effort is futile. A glider does not use an engine. If the aircraft has an engine, it is no longer a glider. Our relationship with God is similar in this sense. Only God can carry us.

We say we are saved by grace alone. What is grace? Grace, by definition, is a free gift. It is not something we can earn through our good works, abilities or possessions. On the contrary, the wages of sin is death (Romans 6:23); by sinning, we earn the consequences – death. The same principle applies to being a disciple of Jesus. Salvation is entirely by grace, not by being good at something. Being a Christian is also by grace; otherwise, we would be no different from the Pharisees. The Pharisees attempted to earn more righteousness through their own resources and effort, but it's an impossible task, so they resorted to pretence – pretending to be righteous while looking down on those who couldn't achieve the same, thus affirming themselves.

The story of the rich young man confronts us with the truth that our possessions, achievements and self-made righteousness can never earn us salvation or bring us closer to God. It challenges our reliance on self-righteousness and worldly measures of spirituality. Jesus calls us to let go of these things and rely solely on Him. We must be aware of the traps of relying on our own resources and recognise that drawing near to God is only possible because of the sacrifice Jesus made on the cross for us.

This truth is not contradictory to the parable of the talents discussed in the previous chapter where we learned about the importance of proactively utilising the resources God has gifted us. The key lies in recognising that not only is everything we own a gift from God, but the yields and fruits we reap are also gifts from God. There is no place for pride and self-righteousness. It is not about doing more but about having less reliance on ourselves. As we embrace the freedom and grace that comes from relinquishing our self-righteousness, may we wholeheartedly rely on God in everything we do.

IV

What is your name?

Setting apart your God-given name from other false names

7

Jacob

In this section, we will look at the idea of God's calling as a name given by God. A name carries expectations and identity. We all have names given to us by our parents. In the Bible, God chose the names of some individuals before they were born (e.g. Ishmael, John the Baptist, Jesus). God also gave new names to those to whom He revealed His calling (e.g. Abraham, Peter). One of the best biblical narratives that sheds light on this notion of calling as a name is the story of God giving Jacob a new name in Genesis 32. Let's return to the story of Esau and Jacob.

As we saw in Chapter 1, the two brothers embodied contrasting extremes. Esau carelessly discarded his birthright, succumbing to immediate pleasures and willingly forfeiting his birthright. Jacob, on the other hand, highly esteemed this privilege, resorting to deceitful means to obtain it. Both Esau and Jacob were driven by their personal desires, relentlessly striving to gratify themselves, ultimately depleting their own lives. How did God address Jacob's relentless pursuits? The famous wrestling scene at the ford of the Jabbok, as recorded in Genesis 32:22–32, gives us some insight.

22 That night Jacob got up and took his two wives, his two female servants and his eleven sons and crossed the ford of the Jabbok. 23 After he had sent them across the stream, he sent over all

his possessions. **24** So Jacob was left alone, and a man wrestled with him till daybreak. **25** When the man saw that he could not overpower him, he touched the socket of Jacob's hip so that his hip was wrenched as he wrestled with the man. **26** Then the man said, "Let me go, for it is daybreak."

But Jacob replied, "I will not let you go unless you bless me."

27 The man asked him, "What is your name?"

"Jacob," he answered.

28 Then the man said, "Your name will no longer be Jacob, but Israel, because you have struggled with God and with humans and have overcome."

29 Jacob said, "Please tell me your name."

But he replied, "Why do you ask my name?" Then he blessed him there.

30 So Jacob called the place Peniel, saying, "It is because I saw God face to face, and yet my life was spared."

31 The sun rose above him as he passed Peniel, and he was limping because of his hip. **32** Therefore to this day the Israelites do not eat the tendon attached to the socket of the hip, because the socket of Jacob's hip was touched near the tendon.

Jacob's struggles resonate with many of us. While Esau dismissed the birthright, Jacob ambitiously sought to seize as much as he could, as if the world owed him everything. In Jacob's view, losing the firstborn position to his twin brother was frustrating. He believed that every opportunity must be seized to obtain it, resorting to luring his older brother with a bowl of stew and deceiving his elderly father by disguising himself with sheepskin on his arms. He planned and strategised, desperately striving to acquire the birthright and the blessings that came with it. Later, in dealing with his uncle Laban, he employed his cunning means again to safeguard his own interests, leading to a series of conflicts. However, years later, just before Jacob encountered Esau once again, God compelled him to confront the issues plaguing his life.

A win-win wrestling match?

Do you know how victors are determined in wrestling matches? Typically, the wrestler who manages to pin the opponent or make the opponent submit will be declared the winner by the referee. But if you were to act as a referee in the wrestling incident at the ford of the Jabbok recorded in Genesis 32, who would you declare as the winner? Would you choose Jacob or God?

It's difficult to declare a clear winner for this bizarre wrestling match. Perhaps it can be seen as a win-win situation, where both parties emerged triumphant but in very different ways. Jacob appeared to be the winner, as the other man realised he could not overpower Jacob (v. 25) and asked to be released (v. 26). The man also proclaimed that Jacob had been victorious in his struggle with both God and man (v. 28). This sounds like a clear victory, doesn't it?

However, the other man, representing God, also had the upper hand. In one swift move, he struck Jacob's hip socket, causing a permanent injury. In a wrestling match, such an injury would immediately bring the match to an end.

Moreover, the man literally changed Jacob's name (v. 28) and blessed him. Both acts were reserved for someone who was significantly superior in status. Finally, while Jacob was compelled to reveal his name, this man did not comply with Jacob's request to reveal his own name.

So then, was Jacob the winner or the loser in this wrestling match? The answer is both. Jacob could be seen as the winner because he successfully attained the blessing he had desperately longed for. However, he walked with a limp for the rest of his life. The limp became a permanent mark of Jacob's incapacity to rely solely on himself. Initially, Jacob believed he could acquire his desires through his own strategies and relying on his own strength. While God was willing to grant him what he desired, Jacob had to learn a lifelong lesson: it was not through his own efforts but through God's mercy. Letting go became his enduring lesson from God. He had to first lose to God in order to triumph. To conquer, one must first surrender.

Genesis underscores this lesson. Throughout Jacob's life, he employed numerous schemes, deceitfully acquiring the birthright from Esau and accumulating considerable wealth from Laban. Yet, in his later years, he encountered a seven-year famine, trading his wealth for sustenance and reluctantly allowing his beloved youngest son, Benjamin, to depart. Eventually, he had no choice but to humble himself and seek refuge with Pharaoh (Genesis 46–47). God intended to instil in Jacob the understanding that everything he endeavoured to gain through his own means would inevitably be lost. God desired to restore everything in Jacob's life, but only on His terms.

A name that defines a calling

In Genesis 32:27, we read,

> The man asked him, "What is your name?"
> "Jacob," he answered.

Why did God inquire about Jacob's name? In the Bible, a person's name often reveals their character. The name Jacob literally means to 'grasp' or to 'supplant' (Genesis 25:26). Since the moment he was born, Jacob's whole life had been about desperately seizing and grasping whatever he viewed as essential to his success. He felt defeated by Esau from birth. Deprived of his father's love due to Isaac's favouritism, Jacob couldn't find a source of security, so he was determined to grasp anything he could.

God wasn't unaware of Jacob's name, but He desired for Jacob to admit it himself so that he could come face-to-face with the reality of his life – a person who spent his life trying to grasp what he wanted. This mirrors the experiences of many of us. Some of us ambitiously strive to compensate for our perceived shortcomings, constantly exerting ourselves and seeking affirmation in everything we do. Personality also plays a role in this dynamic. Introverts may tend to belittle and criticise themselves, while extroverts may resent being outperformed, and strive to be the best. However, regardless of the manifestation, the root cause is often the same as Jacob's: insecurity.

This is diametrically opposed to the notion of trusting God, waiting upon Him and acknowledging that everything we have is a gift from Him. We are accustomed to earning what we want, believing that our hard work will eventually yield the rewards we think we deserve. However, the author of Genesis urges us to ponder a question: did Jacob win or lose in wrestling with God? The answer is multifaceted – he experienced both victory and defeat. It is through loss that one can gain victory.

Letting go is a crucial step in taking up God's calling for us. Jacob had to confront his own failures and acknowledge that what he had been holding onto and striving for could only be granted by God. The same principle applies to our lives, including our calling, gifts, achievements, plans and all that we receive and encounter. They all depend on God's grace alone. Although God can work through our efforts to grant these things, He remains the ultimate source.

In the midst of this encounter and struggle, God granted Jacob two things that profoundly changed his life: a new name and a permanent limp. Let us first explore the significance of the new name.

A new name given by God

> Then the man said, "Your name will no longer be Jacob, but Israel, because you have struggled with God and with humans and have overcome." (Genesis 32:28)

In response to Jacob's old name, God gave him a new name, his true identity. This transformation begins with recognising and acknowledging the original distorted identity. What is the significance of the new name – "Israel" – given to Jacob?

The new name represented not something Jacob has to *do*, but who he *is*. Jacob believed that 'grasping' defined him, a name given by his parents, but he was mistaken. This name didn't truly belong to or define him. Under the new name Israel, God was telling him, "I have chosen you, and you have triumphed in your struggle with God and man. You no longer need to cling to things through your own efforts; instead, you can become a blessing to others." Because of this new identity given by God, Jacob was finally able to let go of all the things he had clung to.

A name represents one's identity and inherent qualities. I recall a teacher who once shared that his calling was to work with troubled youth, guiding them out of confusion and struggles while being a *Faithful Companion* on their journey of growth. He knows this is the name God has given him. Similarly, I have also had the privilege to meet a Christian accountant who shared that his God-given name was *Honest and Upright Accountant*, unwavering in the face of corruption. He doesn't focus on the possibility of losing his job, but solely on fulfilling what God has called him to do. Likewise, I've also met a believer in the insurance industry who expressed that while the industry is all about meeting sales targets, she realised that God's calling for her was not to chase after sales. That wasn't her calling. God gave her a name – *Compassionate Broker* – that entails genuinely looking out for the interests of clients and assisting them in obtaining the best protection for their families.

A name defines a person's identity and purpose. There is a story about a commuter who used a particular train station every day. Each day at the station, he would see a man squatting on the ground with some items and a small plate nearby. One day, seeing the seemingly despondent man and the empty plate, the passenger had pity on him and instinctively took out some cash and placed it on the plate. However, after he walked away, he suddenly realised, "This person is selling his goods, not begging! How did I mistake him for a beggar?" He quickly turned back and apologised, "I'm so sorry! I didn't realise that you were actually a businessman, not a beggar!" He then retrieved his money from the plate.

The passenger never saw the man at that same spot again. Sometime later, while passing through the train station, someone called to him from a shop across the station – it was that same man who used to sell his goods on the ground. The man in the shop said to the passenger, "You were the first person to ever call me a 'businessman'. Your words woke me up. I started taking my business seriously and opened this shop. I am now an official shop owner. I'm truly grateful to you."

Sometimes, all it takes is a name change to transform a person's sense of identity.

What's your God-given name?

We all have many false 'names'

In our lives, our 'names' often turn out to be artificial, bestowed upon us by others. I'm not referring to the names printed on our passports or driver's licences, but the driving force behind the direction of our lives. For instance, we commonly know someone based on their profession, such as teacher, plumber, civil servant and so on. These titles become our names, and we start believing that they define us. However, God's calling is not just about knowing what profession to pursue; it is also about discovering the essence of who God wants us to be in the circumstances in which God has placed us.

Our blind spots and distorted perceptions often prevent us from recognising the multitude of false identities we have adopted, and who we truly are in God. Whether influenced by societal expectations or our own misguided notions, we often live according to other people's standards or those we impose on ourselves. From a young age, we dutifully adhere to our parents' expectations, trying to be good students and believing that academic success defines us. As we start working, social pressures lead us to believe that our job titles are the essence of our identity. Then when we get married, the urge to get onto the property ladder becomes the next drive that shapes our goals and direction. Like Jacob, many believers find themselves living under the weight of false identities, disconnected from God's true calling for their lives.

Whether we want to admit it or not, we place great importance on how others perceive us. Consequently, we allow these expectations to become our names without realising that they are not our true identities. In fact, they may even cause us to miss the true name God has given us.

The truth is that only the name God gives us is our real name.

To know our true name, we must embark on a journey of honest introspection, re-evaluating all the false names we have adopted in the past. This reflection goes beyond the mere positions or roles assigned to us. The new name God has given us is about the qualities and missions God expects us to fulfil within those roles as His children. Teachers may reflect on how God envisions them as educators. Parents need to ask themselves what kind of father or mother God desires them to be, not what society or the extended family expects.

Each person's calling is unique to the individual. There is no set formula. Calling also differs from desire. While they both compel us to work hard, calling acknowledges that all resources are gifts from God, and we should utilise them to fulfil His calling. Desire, on the other hand, seeks self-gratification and self-validation through certain possessions or achievements. It leads to burnout, both physically and mentally, because it is not what we are created for. Such burnout is unnecessary; only God can satisfy and affirm us, and He has already done so. The core message of the story of Jacob wrestling with God is that true satisfaction can only come from God. Jacob needed to align his mindset with this revelation. It became a lifelong lesson for him.

"Please tell me your name."

Our true names only come from our Creator. But sometimes, we want more. In Genesis 32:29, Jacob asked, "Please tell me your name." The other person responded, "Why do you ask my name?" and blessed Jacob there.

Jacob's question about the man's name revealed his persistent tendency to cling and grasp, a characteristic associated with his old name. Despite receiving a new name and a blessing, Jacob still sought to secure more. However, God didn't allow him to succeed.

A similar account can be found in Judges 13:17–18:

> ^{17} Then Manoah enquired of the angel of the Lord, "What is your name, so that we may honour you when your word comes true?" ^{18} He replied, "Why do you ask my name? It is beyond understanding."

Manoah, Samson's father, and his wife were initially unable to conceive a child. God's angel foretold the birth of a son for them. Manoah asked the angel for his name, but the angel refused to disclose it, stating that it was beyond his understanding. God is beyond our grasp.

We often resemble Jacob and Manoah. While acknowledging that all gifts come from God, we still desire to grasp (control) Him. We long to seize God's gifts and blessings, holding them tightly in our hands. However, the manna provided by God in the wilderness serves as a poignant reminder. Each person could only gather enough for the day, not more, as hoarding and self-reliance are explicitly forbidden by God. Our inclination to apply the economic laws of returns to our relationship with God persists, as if our efforts guarantee corresponding outcomes and enable us to manipulate the divine plan. Yet, gifts are not rewards, and they remain outside the realm of our control.

The second commandment of the Ten Commandments directly prohibits the carving of idols among the Israelites. It does not pertain to worshipping other gods, which is already covered in the first commandment. Rather, its focus is on the manner in which the people are to worship the Lord – they must refrain from creating their own idea of God, which is something humans are always inclined to do. This restriction is in place because such an image can be manipulated and controlled, while the Lord Himself cannot be manipulated by humans. All gifts and blessings come from God and cannot be earned, gained or obtained through effort. In the Lord's Prayer, the plea to "Give us today our daily bread" (Matthew 6:11) conveys this idea.

Jacob's life exemplifies this human tendency of clinging tightly, but it also highlights the path to freedom: to receive blessings and a new name from God. This lesson holds true for us as well.

A permanent limp that marks a new life

The passage continues by elaborating on Jacob's limp, specifically mentioning,

> Therefore to this day the Israelites do not eat the tendon attached to the socket of the hip, because the socket of Jacob's hip was touched near the tendon. (v. 32)

Why does the author provide such a detailed description? This is an incredibly painful, devastating injury. Clearly, the intention is to highlight how this experience became an enduring mark on Jacob, serving as a tangible reminder for his descendants. Imagine how Jacob would recall this event every morning as he rose from his bed. All his descendants would also recall this while shopping for groceries at the marketplace as they must avoid buying or consuming tendon. It is a permanent symbol that the whole nation needs to etch in their hearts for generations.

In our lives, we may also have a limp, or something like Paul's thorn in his flesh (2 Corinthians 12:7), that God will not remove. These may be God's imprints through which He intends to teach us important lessons or provide essential reminders. Many believers fear revisiting the past. In particular, they fear confronting regrets and painful experiences, preferring not to reminisce and refusing to acknowledge them. However, just as we reflect on the significance of our own names, it is equally important to re-examine the regrets and experiences in our lives – the losses, failures or traumas we have endured. By doing so, we open ourselves up to God's continuous work in our lives.

By looking back on our past experiences and milestones in life, we may identify moments that stirred our souls and brought us to an encounter with God. Some of us may have responded to God's calling without fully recognising it at the time. Engaging in regular self-reflection enables us to attune our ears to His call. Our character and personality, too, are part of God's creation. Whether we lean towards introversion or extroversion, each person possesses unique strengths and weaknesses. These inherent traits are unchangeable. However, it is crucial for us to ensure that our character does not cloud our receptiveness to His guidance and hamper our understanding of His purpose for our lives.

The gospel, in essence, is about God enabling us to become the person He has always wanted us to be from the very beginning. Our worthiness is not measured by the things we grasp but rather by being who our Creator has called us to be. Never settle for being someone else.

8

The demon-possessed man

Thus far, we have explored various stories in which individuals miss out on living out God's calling because they are consumed by a false sense of self, leading to a distorted understanding and relationship with God. The false self is nothing but deception that robs us of our true self, making us blind to God's plan for our lives. Listening to the voice of the Shepherd is no easy task, as it is often disrupted by alternative voices stemming from our own pride, influences from family and friends, the expectations of our community, and the overwhelming noise of the world around us.

In this chapter, we will look at God's calling in the form of extraordinary redemptive power and mercy in a man whose sense of self has been hopelessly wrecked. The story of the demon-possessed[2] man, with a surprising ending, is recorded in Mark 5:1–20. Let's first consider verses 1–5:

---

[2] The term 'possessed', commonly found in Bible translations including the New International Version (NIV) and the King James Version (KJV), does not denote ownership. Within the context of demonisation, this verb simply signifies "to have a demon or demons". Given that this book primarily references the NIV, it retains the terminology of that translation.

¹ They went across the lake to the region of the Gerasenes. ² When Jesus got out of the boat, a man with an impure spirit came from the tombs to meet him. ³ This man lived in the tombs, and no one could bind him any more, not even with a chain. ⁴ For he had often been chained hand and foot, but he tore the chains apart and broke the irons on his feet. No one was strong enough to subdue him. ⁵ Night and day among the tombs and in the hills he would cry out and cut himself with stones.

This tormented individual, consumed by demons, had been stripped of his freedom, forsaken by society, and had even lost his own sense of identity. He relentlessly inflicted harm upon himself and was trapped in never-ending bondage. Although most of us do not have personal struggles as severe as this man's, there are moments when we too lack self-control, unable to overcome or see any light at the end of the tunnel.

What's your name?

We see various kinds of bondage in modern society as well. When the true self is consumed, controlled and destroyed by something, it is as terrifying as being possessed by demons. Verses 6–9 make this clear:

⁶ When he saw Jesus from a distance, he ran and fell on his knees in front of him. ⁷ He shouted at the top of his voice, "What do you want with me, Jesus, Son of the Most High God? In God's name don't torture me!" ⁸ For Jesus had said to him, "Come out of this man, you impure spirit!"

⁹ Then Jesus asked him, "What is your name?"

"My name is Legion," he replied, "for we are many."

When Jesus asked the man for his name, the response was "Legion". This was clearly not a human name, but a term borrowed from the Roman military structure: a legion consisted of around six thousand soldiers. This was an extreme case of demonic possession. So many demons simultaneously occupying one person undoubtedly wreaked havoc and caused immense devastation. The man was enslaved by demons to the point that his true self was entirely submerged, unable to distinguish between his own identity and that of the demons. Jesus asked for his name to shed light on this hopeless situation. All that remained was the name of the demons. Even in conversation with Jesus, the demons spoke on the man's behalf.

For someone who has lost their true self, the initial step towards recovery is allowing Jesus to ask the fundamental question, "What's your name?" Knowing a person's name is crucial in comprehending their true condition. When God asked Jacob his name at the ford of the Jabbok (Genesis 32:22–32), it served as a reminder to Jacob that his name meant "one who grasps". Through this encounter, Jacob confronted his own struggle and gained a deeper understanding of his reality. Similarly, Jesus's question helped this man realise the extent of his bondage and his hopeless state.

Realisation is the beginning of healing. We often believe that if we can somehow manipulate or control our outward behaviour, we can break free from our problem. Similarly, the residents in Gerasenes held the same belief. They attempted to restrain the man with shackles and iron chains, banishing him to tombs and desolate places, in hopes of resolving the problem. However, this approach proved ineffective.

Consider someone struggling with a gambling addiction. Perhaps they have reached a point where they are disgusted with themselves and yet they are still unable to stop gambling. What truly lies behind this problem? Or take an individual who consistently ruins relationships. It may appear that they lack interpersonal skills, but is that the true source of the problem? All problems in our lives have a much deeper origin than it appears. Jesus accurately identified the issue by revealing the presence of a vast demonic presence inside the man, a presence which had been destroying every aspect of his life.

The story then records three very different requests made to Jesus: (1) the demons pleading with Jesus not to torment them; (2) the people urging Jesus to leave their region; and (3) the man previously possessed by demons requesting to go with Jesus. Let's begin with the first request, found in Mark 5:10–13:

> **10** And he begged Jesus again and again not to send them out of the area.
>
> **11** A large herd of pigs was feeding on the nearby hillside. **12** The demons begged Jesus, "Send us among the pigs; allow us to go into them." **13** He gave them permission, and the impure spirits came out and went into the pigs. The herd, about two thousand in number, rushed down the steep bank into the lake and were drowned.

The first request granted

If we are familiar with the Gospel accounts of Jesus casting out demons, we may notice something unique about this story. The demons pleaded with Jesus, and Jesus seemed to easily accommodate their entreaty, as though submitting to their demands.

Couldn't Jesus have just rebuked and expelled them? Why does this account differ from other accounts of deliverance? In other instances, Jesus displayed much more authority, but here, Jesus granted the demons' plea. The most puzzling part is verse 8: "For Jesus had said to him, 'Come out of this man, you impure spirit!'" The original text reads that Jesus "had already been casting out" demons from the man; however, the passage doesn't specify when Jesus said those words. Why was this man's situation particularly dire?

The demons knew that Jesus intended to drive them out. They knew that they couldn't resist his command. However, they vehemently opposed leaving that area (v. 10). Luke records that they begged Jesus not to send them into the Abyss (see Luke 8:31), which might explain why they earnestly pleaded with Jesus not to torture them (v. 7). Hence, they preferred being sent to a herd of pigs.

Jesus's agreement to send the demons to the pigs demonstrated the destructive power of Legion. Whether it be a human or animals, those under the demons' control will only end up in self-destruction. In a massive herd of two thousand pigs, with each pig possessed by three demons, it was enough to drive them to madness and, ultimately, death.

We can imagine the shock the crowd must have experienced while witnessing two thousand pigs rushing into the sea and drowning. I remember in my childhood seeing trucks carrying live pigs passing through the bustling streets in Hong Kong. Most of the pigs were transported from mainland China, with around ten to twenty pigs crammed onto a single truck. If you can picture one hundred such trucks plunging into the sea, you can grasp how horrific and chaotic the scene would have been. The witnesses must have realised the destructive power of the demons and the terrifying consequences for those under their control.

God chooses mercy above all costs

What happened to the demons after the pigs died? Many readers are curious but the author is not concerned about this. The focus of the story is that Jesus prohibited them from causing further harm to the man he had come to deliver. The passage also highlighted Jesus's compassion. In verse 19, Jesus gave the man a new calling for his life:

> "Go home to your own people and tell them how much the Lord
> has done for you, and how he has had mercy on you."

In order to ensure the man's lasting freedom from the torment of Legion, Jesus was willing to accommodate the demons, even at the cost of sacrificing two thousand pigs. Jesus valued this man's freedom above the opportunity to show off his power.

The only hope we have of being free from any form of struggle in our life, especially addiction, is God's mercy. What the man possessed by demons truly needed was love. Addiction is essentially misguided love. We seek a source of affirmation and eventually become enslaved by it. To break free, there must be an even greater force and an even more compelling source of love. The best and only true solution is to encounter and receive God's love and to be born again.

Some people might wonder, "Isn't it a waste for two thousand pigs to perish without being eaten or sold?" From an economic viewpoint, it was indeed a huge waste. However, from Jesus's perspective, it was not a waste at all; the man's freedom was worth it. Witnessing the sight of two thousand pigs drowning was a visual demonstration for the man that the demons which had tormented him had left and Jesus had set him free.

The second request also granted

Verses 14–17 describe the reaction of the crowd:

> ¹⁴ Those tending the pigs ran off and reported this in the town and countryside, and the people went out to see what had happened. ¹⁵ When they came to Jesus, they saw the man who had been possessed by the legion of demons, sitting there, dressed and in his right mind; and they were afraid. ¹⁶ Those who had seen it told the people what had happened to the demon-possessed man – and told about the pigs as well. ¹⁷ Then the people began to plead with Jesus to leave their region.

The second request in this story came from the people who pleaded with Jesus to leave their region. Surprisingly, Jesus complied once again. We witness a striking contrast between the people and Jesus in how they viewed this situation. One would expect the crowd to be overjoyed at the sight of the man restored to sanity, which would surely have spared them from lots of trouble. Yet instead, they were gripped with fear and begged Jesus to leave them alone. What was the reason for their reaction? The man's restoration had cost them a significant part – perhaps even all – of their livestock. In their eyes, it wasn't worth it.

Gerasenes was a region predominantly inhabited by non-Jews, and pigs were valuable possessions. Every part of a pig was a profitable commodity. The herd of two thousand pigs was of immense value. Some estimates suggest that the herd could have sustained the entire village and served as their primary source of income. This explains why the people were seized with terror and asked Jesus to leave immediately. What kind of society would prefer to sacrifice their entire source of wealth to free one person from bondage? To the people, the man was worthless, nothing more than a nuisance, requiring constant effort to restrain and prevent him from creating havoc. And now, because of him, their economy had been destroyed. The perspective of the people stands in stark contrast to that of Jesus.

The third request denied

The third request came from the protagonist of the story. His request was the best and most reasonable one – to follow Jesus wherever he goes – but shockingly, Jesus rejected it outright! Doesn't Jesus desire everyone to follow him? One possible explanation for this rejection is that if this person followed Jesus and testified in other regions, people would not know the extent of his former wretched state. Consequently, they would not comprehend the great power of God's salvation, particularly His mercy. On the other hand, if he returned to his home town where everyone knew his past, his testimony of God's love would be much more powerful.

However, what is even more profound is Jesus's instruction in verse 19 for this person to go back home:

> "Go home to your own people and tell them how much the Lord has done for you, and how he has had mercy on you."

Facing our past and other people can be a crucial step in our healing process. Consider the loss his fellow townspeople suffered due to the death of the two thousand pigs. They undoubtedly harboured a lot of fear and resentment, making it very challenging for him to face them. Although he had been completely transformed, other people's perceptions and attitudes may not have changed. It would have been easier for the man to move to a foreign land and start a whole new life. Yet, facing his former self and recognising God's mercy and love for him became his calling – to be a living demonstration of God's glory to his own people.

Our past is part of our calling

From this perspective, we can understand the significance of Jesus's command to the man. Confronting past experiences, failures and bondages holds great importance. Jesus desired for this individual to face his past – not to dwell on it, but to gain a clearer vision of God's mercy and the miraculous transformation He had accomplished. The essence of witnessing lies in displaying the living proof of a life transformed from hopelessness into a testimony of grace.

The author of the Gospel of Mark narrates this event with great precision. Apart from mentioning the name "Legion", no other names are provided. The protagonist's actual name is intentionally withheld. How does Mark refer to this person? At the beginning of the passage, he is described as "a man with an impure spirit" (v. 2).

However, after the demons were cast out, the author doesn't assign him a new name. Instead, he continues to refer to him as "the man who had been possessed by the legion of demons" (v. 15) and "the demon-possessed man" (v. 16).

When Jesus was about to leave the region, this man is still referred to as "the man who had been demon-possessed" (v. 18). The repeated use of this lengthy and cumbersome title by the author is not accidental or without purpose. This is the name the Bible wants us to remember.

This person was meant to testify for the Lord, so logically, one would expect his real name to be known. However, his calling became his name. Thus, whenever people mention this person, they would always refer to him as "the man who had been demon-possessed". This negative and clumsy name, despite its lack of appeal, became his powerful testimony for God.

His calling was to embrace his past and boldly proclaim what God had done for him.

In reflecting upon your own life, do you have a name similar to this man's that is attached to your past? Are you "the person who was once ______________" (fill in the blank)? Can you see this is part of Jesus commissioning you to witness for him? Embrace your calling and allow it to become your testimony, confidently declaring the remarkable work of God in your life.

V

Where do you come from?

Recognising where you belong will guide you to where you should go

9

The young Levite

Once upon a time, a handsome man dressed in glamorous clothes was riding on a beautiful horse, gracefully galloping through the forest. Captivated by the sight, a curious onlooker approached him and asked, "Sir, where do you come from?", expecting an extraordinary answer.

The rider replied, "I have no idea. Ask the horse!"

Disappointed by the response, the onlooker asked, "Then where are you going?"

The rider replied, "How would I know? Ask the horse!"

* * *

This is a silly story, but it's an accurate reflection of many people's lives in our society today. After exploring some examples of people in the Bible who missed out on God's calling due to their distorted sense of self or even a loss of self, we will now look at an example of an illusory self in the Old Testament and how it also serves as a tragic antithesis to God's calling. Discerning this illusory self requires a clear understanding of the authentic identity God has intended for us. The only key to unravelling this truth is in the Word of God. Two interesting passages from Judges 17 and 18 shed light on what the authentic self should and should not be.

The story is set against the backdrop of the chaotic period of the Judges, when the Israelites lived in disarray and continuous disobedience. Judges 17 introduces us to Micah, an Ephraimite, who had stolen money from his mother, incurring her curse (this is not the prophet in the book of Micah). He returned the money to his mother, who used a portion of it to fashion an idol for him. Throughout the story, Micah and his mother pursued all kinds of self-serving acts: crafting idols, building a shrine in their home, creating an ephod and other false gods and even appointing a priest to conduct their own rituals. They completely disregarded Yahweh and the Law of Moses. In those days Israel had no king; everyone did as they saw fit (Judges 17:6).

In 17:7–8, another character enters the scene:

> [7] A young Levite from Bethlehem in Judah, who had been living within the clan of Judah, [8] left that town in search of some other place to stay. On his way he came to Micah's house in the hill country of Ephraim.

This young Levite departed from Bethlehem in Judah, wandering around and seeking a new home. When Micah encountered him, he asked:

> "Where are you from?" (v. 9)

Micah's question was simple but significant. When we meet someone for the first time, we usually like to inquire about their origins. The question seemed simple. Yet while the person could have just said, "I come from Bethlehem", he answers instead:

> "I'm a Levite from Bethlehem in Judah… and I'm looking for a place to stay." (v. 9)

This Levite's response contained three parts: "where" – where he came from, "who" – which tribe he belonged to, and "why" – the reason for his presence here.

Since Micah happened to be looking for a Levite to serve as a priest for him, he immediately invited the young Levite to stay with him, promising him financial support, clothing and sustenance (see v. 10). Thus, the Levite became a resident in Micah's household.

The "where", "who" and "what" parts of our identity

This story embodies the essence of the discussion on 'calling' in relation to the true 'self'. For many people, their sense of self is synonymous with where they come from, who they are (their jobs or positions), and what they are currently seeking. Christians are not immune to this. We often use our place of origin, affiliations, occupation or aspirations to define who we are. Micah's response aligned perfectly with these inquiries by offering this confused Levite what he thought was best for him, though it was a position that had absolutely nothing to do with God's original calling for Levites.

A Jewish reader familiar with the Law of Moses would notice something odd about this Levite. A Levite should never be wandering the land; God had given a clear calling to the tribe of Levi. This Levite's answer to the "where" question indicates an identity crisis. According to the Torah, certain cities in the territories of each of the other tribes were designated for Levites to dwell in (Numbers 35:1–8; Joshua 21:1–42; 1 Chronicles 6:54–81). If a city was not designated as a Levitical city, no Levites resided there. Bethlehem was not among the designated cities. The young man's claim of coming from Bethlehem, then, was problematic. No Levite should have identified Bethlehem as his place of origin.

This discrepancy didn't seem to trouble the young man, as he was seeking another place to settle anyway. Though he was a Levite, he strangely had no place to belong, was confused about what he was doing with his life and was wandering the land.

Taking advantage of the Levite's confusion, Micah immediately offered him an invitation to stay with him. This new place would be his home from now on.

As for the question of "who", Micah offered the young man the role of a priest and treated him as a father figure. This was a highly respected position at that time. Yet it also meant that the Levite would no longer serve as a Levite.

Finally, for the "what" aspect, Micah offered him an alternative purpose in life: to receive "ten shekels of silver a year, your clothes and your food" (v. 10). Micah offered him a lucrative job and the prospect of having his material needs met in the future.

This would have been an amazing job offer. However, examining the social and religious context of that time uncovers significant problems in this young Levite's situation. Levites were designated to serve God full-time. They were not allocated land of their own but assigned to live in cities scattered among the other tribes. Each tribe had Levites who were responsible for sacrificial duties. This young man's calling should have been to devote his life to serving the tribe of Judah as a Levite. However, he was apparently resistant to this calling, probably out of dissatisfaction. He abandoned his God-given identity, seeking to be somewhere else and doing something else. The young man quickly became someone else and lost his real identity when an alternative future was presented to him.

What is our authentic self?

This disregard for his true calling and his desperate pursuit of an alternative false calling pose alarming concerns. The young man's decision reflects a genuine temptation to prioritise immediate gratification. Life's path leads to wherever there is better food, higher pay or greater comfort. Sadly, this is how many Christians live today. When we lose our real identity and purpose, the world will quickly offer us appealing alternatives that will drive us further away from God's real calling for our lives.

"Where are you from?" Micah's question is indeed pertinent. This question determines how I see myself, what I should do, how I should do it, what I should pursue and everything else. We need to keep returning to this question because the way we perceive everything else depends on our answer.

The young man was a Levite who should have had a clear role in serving God in a clearly assigned location (Judah). His sacred identity represented a calling from God, and he should have held onto it no matter what. What about you? How do you define your 'self'? Would you also define it based on your place of origin, current occupation and goals? The most important of all, is your answer the same as how God defines you? Or is there a major discrepancy, as with the young man's answer?

I know I come from God. I am a child of God; I am created, chosen, and saved by Him. I am called by Him and redeemed at a great price. I am also a spiritual descendant of Abraham, belonging to God. All these facts impact me; what truly defines my identity is how my Creator sees me. When I say I am a child of God, I am saying that I want to obey God's calling and be the person He wants me to be.

In the book of Judges, the Israelites lacked a meaningful or worthy answer to this question, "Where are you from?" As a result, everyone did as they pleased, going wherever they desired, seeking their own settlements and pursuing personal pleasures. Their primary life pursuits centred around securing the most lucrative positions and the most comfortable lifestyles. In this environment, the most significant questions in life inevitably become "What can I gain? What benefits can I receive?" These are the underlying questions many people seek to answer when planning their careers or building relationships. We are all vulnerable to becoming like the young Levite, losing sight of our true selves and ultimately living a life far away from God's calling.

Who brought you here?

The irony of the story doesn't end here.

In Judges 18:1, the story continues:

> In those days Israel had no king. And in those days the tribe of the Danites was seeking a place of their own where they might

> settle, because they had not yet come into an inheritance among the tribes of Israel.

This passage reveals that the pathetic situation of the young Levite wasn't limited solely to an individual; it also symbolized the plight of the tribe of Dan. Despite the allocation of land to the tribes, their lack of faith prevented them from conquering their enemies and occupying the territory. Instead, they wandered around in search of a place to dwell. In verses 2–4:

> [2] So the Danites sent five of their leading men from Zorah and Eshtaol to spy out the land and explore it. These men represented all the Danites. They told them, "Go, explore the land."
>
> So they entered the hill country of Ephraim and came to the house of Micah, where they spent the night. [3] When they were near Micah's house, they recognised the voice of the young Levite; so they turned in there and asked him, "Who brought you here? What are you doing in this place? Why are you here?"
>
> [4] He told them what Micah had done for him, and said, "He has hired me and I am his priest."

The tribe dispatched spies to find a suitable dwelling place. The spies encountered the young Levite. Recognising that he wasn't an Ephraimite, they bombarded him with questions: "How did you end up here? Who made you come here? What are you doing here?" (paraphrase of v. 3).

This set of questions merely restates Micah's initial question, addressing the same underlying issue regarding the Levite's condition.

"Who brought you here?" Many people find their lives being steered by job prospects, parents' expectations, other people's opinions or the mortgage payments on a house. The young Levite was no exception. Micah offered him better compensation than what he had in Bethlehem in Judah, so he immediately agreed to stay with him. A worry-free income and a comfortable life became his god and his false calling. The questions "What are you doing in this place? Why are you here?" are essentially asking "Who owns you?" No one can avoid these fundamental questions in life. They will continue to haunt us throughout our lives until we find the right answer.

The young Levite then sought guidance through divination on behalf of the five spies and told them their "journey has the Lord's approval" (18:6). The spies then returned with six hundred armed men to invade the land, as detailed in verses 18–20:

> **18** When the five men went into Micah's house and took the idol, the ephod and the household gods, the priest said to them, "What are you doing?"
>
> **19** They answered him, "Be quiet! Don't say a word. Come with us, and be our father and priest. Isn't it better that you serve a tribe and clan in Israel as priest rather than just one man's household?"
>
> **20** The priest was very pleased. He took the ephod, the household gods and the idol and went along with the people.

The young Levite was offered another job and another identity. This is like the third temptation the Devil gave to Jesus as he showed him the splendour of the world on the top of the mountain – "All this I will give you . . . if you will bow down and worship me" (Matthew 4:9). The young Levite yearned to be the priest of an entire tribe, a whole clan. This was not because he cared about the spiritual needs of the people; this was surely not what God had called a Levite from Bethlehem to do. The allure of the opportunities presented by these Danite men was evidently more enticing than what Micah had to offer. The young Levite, who was concerned only with what was most advantageous and prestigious, immediately fell for the new offer and took up another identity. Of the options presented to him, he simply chose the name and fortune that held greater appeal in the moment. A person living with an illusory sense of self can be quickly swayed in any direction.

The death of the illusory self

Many people spend their lives pursuing what they perceive as their true selves and end up being enslaved by their pursuits, exchanging their Creator for a lesser god and forgetting what truly matters. This was precisely the situation of the Israelites during the period covered by the book of Judges. The author repeatedly asserts: "In those days, Israel had no king; everyone did as they saw fit" (see 17:6, 18:1, 21:25). In reality, the Lord should have been their king.

Are we in the same situation? Do we live our lives as we see fit? When the world confronts us with the questions, "Where do you come from? Who brought you here? What are you doing here?" and presents us with lucrative options that contradict God's will, are we able to respond with conviction and clarity and express the calling God has given us?

Let us remember that living out our true self requires the killing of the illusory self. Otherwise, we are no different from the young Levite, a spiritual chameleon. Once we have identified where we come from and who our boss truly is, we will no longer live arbitrarily. The calls of this world, other people's expectations, and life's circumstances around you will lose their hold on you. The true self demands that it be so.

Let us continuously return to the question "Where are you from?" and ensure that our answer aligns with God's truth.

10

Isaiah

As we saw in the previous chapter, the question "Where are you from?" is a fundamental starting point for discerning God's calling for our lives. Only by having a clear answer to this question can we clearly see where we should be going. This is why having a solid biblical understanding of God's creation as depicted in Genesis 1–2 is of paramount importance in how we understand the rest of the Bible, and hence, who we are in God.

Churches today place significant emphasis on preaching about salvation and redemption through the work of Jesus on the cross. By contrast, there is much less focus on teaching the concept and theology of creation. As a result, we may lack a comprehensive understanding of our relationship with God. The concept of creation significantly influences our understanding of our identity and calling. While redemption focuses on the restoration and reconciliation of our broken relationship with God, creation theology focuses on the original relationship God intended between Himself and humankind. To fully grasp God's calling in every aspect of our lives – our work, relationships, ministries and more – we must first understand what it means to be a human being according to the teachings of the Bible. This foundational understanding begins with an exploration of Genesis 1 and 2. After all, we are all created by God in His image, and our lives are an integral part of His creation. God doesn't only care about our afterlife in heaven, but also our current life on earth, where everything is a product of His creative work. The recurring phrase "under the sun," frequently found throughout the Old Testament book of Ecclesiastes, underscores this very point.

How creation defines who we are

We can gain insight into God's calling for us through the lens of creation as it reveals how God envisions His relationship with His creation. The book of Isaiah, specifically in 45:1–11, can shed some light on this matter.

This passage highlights how God created a person – King Cyrus of Persia. Following the downfall of Judah and the exile of the Israelites, who endured years of hardship and captivity, God intends to lead them back to their homeland. How does He plan to achieve this? God uses King Cyrus as an instrument to deliver His people, but Cyrus is unaware that he is being used by God as a tool to carry out His divine purpose in history.

At that time, Babylon was so powerful that no one could have anticipated that the Jewish people would be allowed to leave Babylon and return home. The Babylonians possessed advanced technology, unrivalled innovations and an expanding dominion. In comparison, Cyrus and his Persian empire seemed inferior. It was only through God's plan and accomplishment, as stated in Scripture, that the Israelites escaped Babylon's grasp through Cyrus. Let us first examine Isaiah 45:1–3:

> ¹ This is what the Lord says to his anointed,
>   to Cyrus, whose right hand I take hold of
>   to subdue nations before him
>   and to strip kings of their armour,
>   to open doors before him
>   so that gates will not be shut:
> ² I will go before you
>   and will level the mountains;

> I will break down gates of bronze
> and cut through bars of iron.
> ³ I will give you hidden treasures,
> riches stored in secret places,
> so that you may know that I am the Lord,
> the God of Israel, who summons you by name.

Despite being a Gentile, Cyrus is anointed and empowered by God, who takes hold of his right hand, strengthens him and strips kings of their armour (see v. 1), preparing the way for him because he is the person God has called by name (see v. 4). This embodies the concept of our Creator's sovereignty: God calling and appointing individuals. The notion of God's calling is intertwined with creation throughout the Bible. In the first chapter of Genesis, God's act of creation includes naming, such as designating light as "day" and darkness as "night". Names represent a person's qualities and identity.

In the Hebrew worldview, before God created a person, He already had specific intentions for that individual. God's plan was not limited to the Hebrew people. In the case of Cyrus in Isaiah 45, God had a specific purpose for him – to defeat Babylon and deliver Israel from turmoil. After creating Cyrus, God called him by name, summoning him to fulfil the role God had assigned him. Cyrus was created by God, as part of God's predetermined plan.

Even though Cyrus didn't acknowledge or revere God, God still called and appointed him to fulfil His mission. The fundamental concept of calling aligns with the concept of creation. God created each person, and He has unique intentions and purpose for each one. Even when individuals sin and disobey God, God's mercy and plans cannot be foiled, and His grace is not compromised. His purposes will be fully accomplished, just as His redemption plan was never thwarted by Judas's betrayal of Jesus.

Isaiah 45:4 states,

> For the sake of Jacob my servant, of Israel my chosen,
>   I summon you by name and bestow on you a title of honour,
>   though you do not acknowledge me.

God chose Cyrus not because He desired to elevate him to greatness or because of any remarkable qualities Cyrus possessed. Rather, it was entirely driven by God's overarching plan for His chosen people. While Cyrus may not have had personal knowledge of God, the Lord still gave him a name and called him by it. Herein lies the profound distinction between creation and redemption: not every individual repents or responds to Jesus's redemption. However, every person, without exception, is created by God in His image and is a recipient of His foundational grace of creation.

Isaiah 45:5–6 then stresses,

> [5] I am the Lord, and there is no other;
>   apart from me there is no God.
>   I will strengthen you,
>   though you have not acknowledged me,
> [6] so that from the rising of the sun
>   to the place of its setting
>   people may know there is none besides me.
>   I am the Lord, and there is no other.

God wanted Cyrus to understand that his ability to defeat Babylon had nothing to do with his own abilities, but everything to do with God's sovereignty and working behind the scenes. God raised Cyrus and placed him in this time of history with a purpose – to make people acknowledge that He alone is Lord. The passage affirms that God's creation is purposeful.

What does this mean to all of us? We must know with absolute certainty that God passionately yearns for us and is ever-present to guide us into becoming the individuals He designed us to be. Once we grasp this fundamental truth, we can wholeheartedly devote ourselves to His calling, embrace our identity in God and overcome all kinds of challenges and difficulties.

Whose sovereignty?

Isaiah 45:7–10 introduces another concept, highlighting God's sovereignty:

> 7 I form the light and create darkness,
>   I bring prosperity and create disaster;
>   I, the Lord, do all these things.
> 8 You heavens above, rain down my righteousness;
>   let the clouds shower it down.
>   Let the earth open wide,
>   let salvation spring up,
>   let righteousness flourish with it;
>   I, the Lord, have created it.
> 9 Woe to those who quarrel with their Maker,
>   those who are nothing but potsherds
>   among the potsherds on the ground.
>   Does the clay say to the potter,
>   "What are you making?"
>   Does your work say, "The potter has no hands"?
> 10 Woe to the one who says to a father,
>   "What have you begotten?"
>   or to a mother,
>   "What have you brought to birth?"

In Old Testament times, light and darkness often symbolised blessings and afflictions. Both peace and calamity come from God, forming integral parts of His creation. As depicted in Genesis chapter 1, God first created light, leaving one to assume that His creation would exist in perpetual brightness. Yet, His creation took a different turn: instead of eliminating darkness, He separated light from it, enabling both light and darkness, day and night, to coexist while separated (even before the fall). Isaiah also points this out, stating: "I form the light and create darkness, I bring prosperity and create disaster; I, the Lord, do all these things" (v. 1)

The ups and downs of life mirror this duality. While we often imagine God's creation to be perfect, it's important to remember that only God Himself is perfect. Many believers assume God's creation must have been perfect originally. They find it challenging to accept the fact that there are trials that God allows them to endure. They question why their lives are fraught with hardship, and why God bestows both blessings and suffering. Yet Genesis never implies the material world described in Genesis 1–2 was intended to be eternal; indeed, it is merely transitory, comprising light and darkness, blessings and afflictions. Those who are familiar with the book of Job know that receiving blessings and having them taken away are both under God's sovereignty. Although many find this perplexing, God's sovereign creation entails these contrasts.

In our calling, too, we encounter things that we cannot fully understand. Yet, viewed from the perspective of creation, it's not surprising that our calling may include both blessings and afflictions, highs and lows, joys and sorrows. Afflictions can, indeed, be part of our calling. Some people may spend a significant portion of their lives bemoaning their circumstances, questioning God's intentions and thereby failing to fulfil His plan for them. Scripture assures us that everything, even the incomprehensible, is part of God's creation and under His control.

For instance, in Isaiah 45:8, righteousness and rain symbolise blessings. They depict a scene of heavenly shower refreshing the earth. Despite life's hardships, we need not fear, as God's grace is abundant and sufficient. All things, good and bad, are created by God and fall under His control. We don't need to know all the answers to put our trust in God.

Isaiah 45:9–10 reiterates God's sovereignty. It portrays created beings who are discontent with their form and challenge their Maker. The analogy of a potter and clay underscores God's sovereignty. The verses assert that everything God creates has value and is inherently good. The potter is the boss.

Today, we should appraise the worth of our lives not by our monetary gains, achievements, or societal contributions, but by our innate value in being His creation. Genesis 1–2 tells us that it is God who decides what is good. We are valuable to God because He says so. The story of creation is closely linked to our lives and experiences, and it teaches us that every person, no matter how insignificant they might feel, is precious.

The ultimate comfort for the created

Isaiah 45:11 states:

> This is what the Lord says –
>> the Holy One of Israel, and its Maker:
>> concerning things to come,
> do you question me about my children,
>> or give me orders about the work of my hands?

Basically, God was saying, "Everything is on Me!" The preceding verses discuss the meaning, sovereignty, and significance in God's creation, and here reveals the ultimate comfort for the created. The Israelites' situation at that time was bleak – generations had been oppressed and they were now morally corrupt, and the restoration of their nation seemed impossible. However, God was telling them, "You are my creation, my people. I will do as I please with you. I will take care of everything; everything is under my control."

In today's postmodern world, belief in unlimited freedom and self-definition is prevalent. A common motto is, "You can become whoever you want to be." While empowering, this self-deceiving message often brings people anxiety and disappointment when they don't meet their own expectations. True freedom and peace, however, aren't found in boundless autonomy but within the boundaries and purpose set by God. Living within God's design is the most secure path because we can trust that He will always bring to fruition His plans for us. This promise is the ultimate source of comfort and confidence.

In summary, this passage in Isaiah provides us with at least three reminders about who we are as God's creation:

1. Created for God: Our lives are prepared for God. He created us, and each one of us has a unique purpose.
2. Created according to God: We are created according to God's sovereignty and values; our worth is determined by Him. What is good and what is not good are defined by God.
3. Created by God: We are covered by God's provision. He will accomplish everything and take care of everything for us.

The design and gift of creation

Notice how this passage in Isaiah mirrors the account in Genesis 1:

1. God's creation includes naming what He created, "God called . . . ", representing the qualities, functions and meanings assigned by God to what he has created.
2. Throughout the six days of creation, the repetition of "God said . . . " (vv. 3, 6, 9, 11, 14, 20, 24, 26, 29) stresses God's sovereignty. Whatever He desires, He brings into existence according to His commands. The passage also repeatedly highlights, "God saw that it was good" (vv. 4, 10, 12, 18, 21, 25, 31), indicating that the value of everything is determined by God.
3. God's creation did not end with its completion; He also "blessed" it (vv. 22, 28), endowing the created beings with abilities to fulfil His purposes. God's intentions for us are accompanied by His blessings, and He will personally accomplish them.

Genesis 1 illustrates how God set apart light from darkness, as well as distinguish between creatures in the air, the sea and the land. These symbolise boundaries God has set for the material world. However, we dislike boundaries and being restricted by someone else, and the book of Ecclesiastes reflects this lack of satisfaction. This material world cannot provide true contentment to us; only what is eternal can. Yet, as Genesis 2 emphasises, this present world is also a gift from God.

In fact, every aspect of God's design is a gift He intends for us, our calling included. His benevolent gifts underscore the profound significance and value of our existence, as envisioned and endowed by our Creator. Therefore, as created beings, understanding God's intentions in our creation and responding to His call forms the bedrock of our faith. Today, our purpose and the meaning of our existence are rooted in becoming the individuals God intended us to be.

God has been calling us since the beginning

The book of Isaiah continues to provide comforting words to God's people by reminding them of God's calling and faithfulness to us even before our birth. Later in chapter 49, a powerful illustration is presented (Isaiah 49:1-6):

> ¹ Listen to me, you islands;
>> hear this, you distant nations:
>> before I was born the Lord called me;
>> from my mother's womb he has spoken my name.
> ² He made my mouth like a sharpened sword,
>> in the shadow of his hand he hid me;
>> he made me into a polished arrow
>> and concealed me in his quiver.
> ³ He said to me, "You are my servant,
>> Israel, in whom I will display my splendour."
> ⁴ But I said, "I have laboured in vain;
>> I have spent my strength for nothing at all.
>> Yet what is due to me is in the Lord's hand,

and my reward is with my God."
⁵ And now the Lord says –
  he who formed me in the womb to be his servant
  to bring Jacob back to him
  and gather Israel to himself,
  for I am honoured in the eyes of the Lord
  and my God has been my strength –
⁶ he says:
  "It is too small a thing for you to be my servant
  to restore the tribes of Jacob
  and bring back those of Israel I have kept.
  I will also make you a light for the Gentiles,
  that my salvation may reach to the ends of the earth."

The passage begins with a reflection on the most fundamental question about our identity – "Where do we come from?" Being formed and established from the womb highlights the fact that our calling from God, our divine calling, is ordained even before our birth. We must understand that our true identity has nothing to do with our deeds or achievements today but has everything to do with who formed us in the womb (v. 4). In times of adversity, it is crucial to remain steadfast in our identity and anchor ourselves in this understanding, remembering that we were chosen by God even before our first breath and placed in specific positions for a purpose.

Additionally, verse 3 depicts us as God's servants, which carries a deeper meaning than mere workers. In ancient times, servants held the esteemed role of ambassadors, representing the will and authority of the masters. As God's servants, we play these same sacred roles. It's vital to internalise our status as God's cherished children, called to bring honour and glory to Him.

As chapter 49 unfolds, the Israelites voice their frustrations. We witness the Israelites expressing their discontent and feeling that their efforts are in vain. They question their status as God's chosen servants. However, in response, God reminds them that He's the one who formed them from the womb to be His servants (v. 5). God doesn't abandon His chosen ones but uses hardships and challenges to mould them into instruments of His will. He calls them to be His representatives.

This comforting message isn't confined to the Israelites, but speaks to each of us today. From the beginning, God has been calling us, preparing us to fulfil a unique purpose. We must recognise our sacred identity as His chosen ambassadors. We are shining lights in a dark world. We belong to Him.

The book of Isaiah presents a powerful message of God's calling throughout history. May we heed His call, embrace our identity and live our lives for His purpose with unwavering faith.

VI

Whose expectation is it?

Discerning false expectations from a false boss

11

Balaam

Throughout the Bible, we encounter individuals who have found themselves at the crossroads of the unwavering calling of God and the alluring alternative voices of the world. Indeed, Christians can be caught in the same dilemma today in the professional marketplace. Balaam, a well-known diviner and prophet in the book of Numbers, is a striking and tragic example of this dilemma. His story provides us with insights into the perils of a distorted sense of calling as well as God's faithfulness to the people He called. In this chapter, we will look at the fascinating story of Balaam (and his talking donkey) as we explore calling in the face of conflicting desires and expectations.

The book of Numbers dedicates three whole chapters to Balaam's story (chapters 22–24). The Israelites had arrived at the plains of Moab, and the Moabite king offered the prophet Balaam generous rewards to curse the Israelites. In Numbers 22:6, King Balak of Moab instructed Balaam:

> "Now come and put a curse on these people, because they are too powerful for me. Perhaps then I will be able to defeat them and drive them out of the land. For I know that whoever you bless is blessed, and whoever you curse is cursed."

However, God's will was not to curse the Israelites but to bless them.

Throughout the Old Testament, starting from the story of Adam and Eve, you can see God's steadfast refusal to curse His people. Here, God forbade Balaam to curse them by obstructing him at every turn. Yet Balaam still coveted the rewards offered by Balak and sought to fulfil his request by any means necessary. As a result, he became merely a vain puppet of God's enemy.

Whose calling should I follow?

In Numbers 22:8, Balaam pathetically tried to please his client:

> "Spend the night here," Balaam said to them, "and I will report back to you with the answer the Lord gives me." So the Moabite officials stayed with him.

Balaam knew that King Balak's request involved Yahweh, the God of the Israelites. He had no choice but to seek Yahweh's counsel first. This may seem to display great piety. However, he was not a true prophet at all; if he had been, he would have known God's heart and would have rejected outright Balak's request to curse God's people. Balaam was not a prophet of the Israelites like Isaiah or Jeremiah. He was more like a secular diviner and a celebrity fortune-teller. Even the Moabite king had heard of him. Professional sorcerers, who engaged in divination and communication with various spirits through what is known as spiritism, considered every deity to be their object of service or a business tool.

Balaam may have had frequent success in contacting various deities. He believed that if God granted his request, then his attempt to curse the Israelites would surely succeed. Balaam successfully contacted Israel's God; however, God plainly responded:

> "Do not go with them. You must not put a curse on those people, because they are blessed." (Numbers 22:12)

Thus, the next morning, Balaam informed Balak's messengers: "Go back to your own country, for the Lord has refused to let me go with you" (v. 13). In verses 15 to 19, we see Balak's dissatisfaction with this refusal:

> ¹⁵ Then Balak sent other officials, more numerous and more distinguished than the first. ¹⁶ They came to Balaam and said: "This is what Balak son of Zippor says: do not let anything keep you from coming to me, ¹⁷ because I will reward you handsomely and do whatever you say. Come and put a curse on these people for me." ¹⁸ But Balaam answered them, "Even if Balak gave me all the silver and gold in his palace, I could not do anything great or small to go beyond the command of the Lord my God. ¹⁹ Now spend the night here so that I can find out what else the Lord will tell me."

The original text does not contain the possessive pronoun "my" in "the command of the Lord my God" in verse 18. Balaam wasn't acknowledging Yahweh as *his* Lord. And even if "my" had been included, it wouldn't indicate that Balaam was a true prophet. To diviners like Balaam, God was just one of the many deities they needed to contact for their jobs. Deities were vital service suppliers. Now, an important client (Balak) had come to request the cursing of the Israelites. It was only natural for Balaam to consult the deity who governed this people group. His client was his boss.

To be clear, Balaam wasn't seeking Yahweh's counsel out of reverence for Him. He knew very well that a curse on the Israelites would not be effective because their God, Yahweh, had already warned him not to curse them. If his prophecies did not come true, his reputation would be ruined. His entire career were at stake. To maintain an appearance of 'professionalism' for his continuous success and fame, Balaam realised he had to refuse this risky business deal.

However, King Balak was not willing to give up easily. He was willing to increase the price and even promised to do whatever Balaam wanted in return (v. 17), hoping to change Balaam's mind. Although Balaam initially refused, deep down in his heart he desired the handsome reward and the golden career opportunity. Therefore, he resorted to a delaying tactic: "Now spend the night here so that I can find out what else the Lord will tell me" (v. 19).

Balaam knew that the Lord wouldn't permit him to curse the Israelite people, and he knew he couldn't force it, but he still wanted to try again nonetheless, hoping that Yahweh would somehow give him a more favourable answer. That way, he could close the deal. Ultimately, Balaam's calculations were driven by greed.

The sign of a talking donkey

In verses 20 to 24, an interesting turn of event happens:

> **20** That night God came to Balaam and said, "Since these men have come to summon you, go with them, but do only what I tell you."
>
> **21** Balaam got up in the morning, saddled his donkey and went with the Moabite officials. **22** But God was very angry when he went, and the angel of the Lord stood in the road to oppose him. Balaam was riding on his donkey, and his two servants were with him. **23** When the donkey saw the angel of the Lord standing in the road with a drawn sword in his hand, it turned off the road into a field. Balaam beat it to get it back on the road. **24** Then the angel of the Lord stood in a narrow path through the vineyards, with walls on both sides.

Initially, God seemed to allow Balaam to go and do what he wanted, but at the same time, He was furious at Balaam. This may seem contradictory, but it can be understood. God knew how hard Balaam's heart was and how unwilling he was to give up. He allowed Balaam to proceed but demanded that he obey God's command. God's intention might have been: "Since you clearly understand My will, you should know that no matter how many times you ask, it will be in vain. However, if you still want to preserve your professional status, then go and speak according to My instructions."

Thus, Balaam set out with the Moabite messengers, hoping that there might still be some room for change. However, God did not approve of his actions and hindered him on the way through supernatural means – a talking donkey.

Many modern readers consider this story unbelievable; a talking donkey only appears in fairy tales. It's too implausible! However, if we understand the cultural background of that time, we will realise that the text made perfect sense to ancient readers. Sorcerers and oracles like Balaam used various methods to discern the will of the gods, and one commonly used method was observing the condition and behaviour of animals. Archaeologists have found evidence of such practices, and the Bible also records instances where animals were sacrificed, and the colour of their livers examined as a means of decision-making (see Ezekiel 21:21). There were many similar methods of seeking answers based on the behaviour of animals.

Balaam, as a professional oracle, should have been sensitive to super-natural signs and visions displayed by animals. In his culture, a talking animal was an important sign from deities. His donkey's continuous and strange behaviour should have been a very clear warning from heaven. An experienced sorcerer should have understood the significance of these signs and realised God was warning him not to proceed further. His contemporaries would have regarded the act of striking the donkey three times before turning back as both unnecessary and unprofessional. However, because of his obsession with the pursuit of Balak's rewards, even his professional sensibilities were clouded. This is what the author is trying to highlight in the text. While the notion of a talking donkey may seem unbelievable to modern readers, the passage is intended to help us see the ridiculous level of Balaam's folly and stubbornness.

Balaam's pursuit of vanity was exceptional. Even though his professional instincts should have alerted him that things would not work out, he persisted in his disobedience, unwilling to give up, and determined to achieve his desires at all costs. He had chosen to fear an earthly king more than the King of the Universe, and had become a hopeless, laughable figure in front of both his client and God. He offered sacrifices at three different locations, attempting to manipulate the situation, believing that by offering more sacrifices to God, God might change His mind and no longer hinder him from clinching this business deal.

However, three times he failed to curse the Israelites; instead, blessings for Israel were uttered. In the end, God permitted him to proceed, not to curse Israel, but to bless them.

The shocking ending and a sobering lesson

This story should have had a happy and victorious ending for the Israelite people. God had miraculously shielded His people through divine protection and providence from their enemy's curses. However, the story is not yet over, and the most alarming part is yet to come.

In Numbers 25:1–9, the narrative suddenly shifts to another event, describing how the Israelites turned to worship Baal at Peor, resulting in God's wrath:

> [1] While Israel was staying in Shittim, the men began to indulge in sexual immorality with Moabite women, [2] who invited them to the sacrifices to their gods. The people ate the sacrificial meal and bowed down before these gods. [3] So Israel yoked themselves to the Baal of Peor. And the Lord's anger burned against them. [4] The Lord said to Moses, "Take all the leaders of these people, kill them and expose them in broad daylight before the Lord, so that the Lord's fierce anger may turn away from Israel."
>
> [5] So Moses said to Israel's judges, "Each of you must put to death those of your people who have yoked themselves to the Baal of Peor." [6] Then an Israelite man brought into the camp a Midianite woman right before the eyes of Moses and the whole assembly of Israel while they were weeping at the entrance to the tent of

meeting. [7] When Phinehas son of Eleazar, the son of Aaron, the priest, saw this, he left the assembly, took a spear in his hand [8] and followed the Israelite into the tent. He drove the spear into both of them, right through the Israelite man and into the woman's stomach. Then the plague against the Israelites was stopped; [9] but those who died in the plague numbered 24,000.

The tragic change was instigated by Balaam, as we can understand from two passages in the New Testament. In 2 Peter 2:15–16:

[15] They have left the straight way and wandered off to follow the way of Balaam son of Bezer, who loved the wages of wickedness. [16] But he was rebuked for his wrongdoing by a donkey – an animal without speech – who spoke with a human voice and restrained the prophet's madness.

Revelation 2:14:

"Nevertheless, I have a few things against you: There are some among you who hold to the teaching of Balaam, who taught Balak to entice the Israelites to sin so that they ate food sacrificed to idols and committed sexual immorality."

Knowing that cursing the Israelites would be futile, Balaam devised a wicked scheme to incite the Israelites to worship Baal. This would lead to the downfall of the Israelites for abandoning God, and he would finally receive his payment from Balak. We can understand this from the New Testament references. Balaam never bore a grudge against the Israelites, nor did he particularly hate this nation. However, he made every effort to curse them, driven by his desire for the attractive wealth his client offered. Such extreme vanity of the heart is truly terrifying. In 2 Peter 2:15, Balaam is described as loving "the wages of wickedness", which accurately captures this aspect of Balaam's condition.

It turns out that the Israelites' biggest enemy wasn't King Balak or any external powers after all. No one could bring a curse or harm upon God's people except themselves. Nothing except their own sins and pride could remove God's blessings. This is a sobering reminder for all Christians.

The real adversary, as the Israelites' story teaches us, resides within us. Yielding to temptation, as the Israelites did with Baal worship, or surrendering to greed and vanity, as Balaam did, paves the way for our downfall. If our inner selves are swayed by our desires and clouded by our ambitions, we may find ourselves drifting away from God's calling, becoming our own most formidable adversary.

When it comes to discerning God's calling, many Christians worry about not hearing God clearly enough or overlooking 'signs' from God. Balaam heard God's voice loud and clear and even witnessed the wonders of a talking donkey, but his selfish desires still compelled him to repeatedly disobey. Some Christians also worry about attacks from the Enemy or hindrances from other people. None of these is the main problem in this story. God's protection and faithfulness trump them all. The only thing that can hinder us from following God's calling is our own sins and pride. The only one we need to be vigilantly guarding ourselves from is ourselves.

The journey of answering God's calling, although marked with challenges and obstacles, shouldn't inspire fear. External difficulties lose their power in the face of a gracious and mighty God. Our vigilance should be primarily directed inward. We must guard against becoming like the Israelites, succumbing to temptation; or the wavering prophet Balaam, driven and blinded by earthly desires. God's divine calling is loud and clear in Scripture. Often, it's our misguided selves that stand in the way. When we don't fear God, we end up fearing other things and other people. When we don't adhere to God's calling, we end up as a powerless puppet, following other people's callings.

As we conclude this chapter, let us reflect on our own hearts. Each of us is at a crossroads between God's calling and alternative callings from this world. It takes a vigilant heart to discern the conflicting callings in our lives. It takes commitment to align our will with God's heart.

12

Amos

For young Christians in the workforce, the concept of calling may resonate with questions about vocational choices and career paths, a subject that holds great significance for them. While Scripture may not provide a prescriptive path for every Christian's professional journey, the Bible clearly emphasises the value God places on our everyday work. God cares deeply about how we do our work, as well as our attitudes and perspectives, because it is also part of His calling. How do we view work? This question is crucial.

Whether in the marketplace or in Christian ministries, every Christian has a role that matters deeply in God's eyes. Having explored the story of Balaam, who tragically heeded a worldly calling over God's calling in his profession, this chapter shifts its focus to celebrate a victorious example: Amos.

Amos 7:10–17 features an intriguing conversation between two biblical figures representing two radically different views of work, from which we can gain significant insights as we reflect on our work. Let's first examine verses 10 to 13:

> ¹⁰ Then Amaziah the priest of Bethel sent a message to Jeroboam king of Israel: "Amos is raising a conspiracy against you in the very

> heart of Israel. The land cannot bear all his words. [11] For this is what Amos is saying: "'Jeroboam will die by the sword, and Israel will surely go into exile, away from their native land.'"
>
> [12] Then Amaziah said to Amos, "Get out, you seer! Go back to the land of Judah. Earn your bread there and do your prophesying there. [13] Don't prophesy anymore at Bethel, because this is the king's sanctuary and the temple of the kingdom."

As an older contemporary of Isaiah, Amos lived around the 8th century BC when the nation was divided into two: the southern kingdom of Judah, ruled by Rehoboam, with Jerusalem as its capital, and the northern kingdom of Israel, ruled by Jeroboam, with Bethel as its centre of worship. Verse 10 tells us that Amaziah was the priest of Bethel, representing the northern kingdom. Amos, on the other hand, was from the southern kingdom of Judah, but God sent him as a prophet to the northern kingdom to deliver His messages to the people there.

This was an incredibly difficult task. At that time, the two kingdoms were hostile towards each other. It was viewed as inappropriate for Amos, as a representative of the southern kingdom, to prophesy in the northern kingdom. To make it worse, the message from God was an extremely negative one: it not only predicted Jeroboam's death by the sword, but also declared that God would punish the northern kingdom, and that the people would be destroyed and exiled. One can imagine how unpleasant and unwelcome these words were to the subjects of the northern kingdom. However, speaking these unwelcome words was Amos's calling from God.

Spiritual battles in the workplace

Some Christians have a tendency to classify different professions into spiritual ranks, with pastors seemingly more sacred than other occupations, and missionaries more esteemed than pastors. The next level may include service-based professions such as doctors, nurses, teachers, social workers, and so on. The least 'spiritual' ones are usually those in businesses, as they are often seen as profit-oriented. Such classification is not found in the Bible. In this story, we have a priest and a prophet, both sacred professions at the time. However, their perspectives on their professions couldn't be more different. Let's explore their contrasts.

Amaziah, the priest from the northern kingdom, revealed a lot about his attitude to his work in his speech (vv. 10–13). He saw it merely as a job. First and foremost, in his eyes, Amos had made a terrible professional mistake by coming to someone else's territory and bad-mouthing the leader and the whole population, saying things that shouldn't be spoken. Amos was ruining his future and committing professional suicide, "because this is the king's sanctuary and the temple of the kingdom" (v. 13). He should have uttered those prophecies back in the southern kingdom of Judah, where plenty of people would have loved to hear about the northern kingdom's destruction.

Amaziah stressed the importance of location. Both verses 12 and 13 focus on location: "Go back to the land of Judah. Earn your bread there and do your prophesying there. Don't prophesy anymore at Bethel." He was warning Amos: if you have to speak, go speak where you'll be popular.

If prophesying was merely a profitable job, then Amaziah's comments make sense. In such a politically sensitive time, Amos's message entangled him in political turmoil. His words sounded like a conspiracy to overthrow the state, making them highly offensive.

Work may be idolatry in disguise

This is not solely an ancient political problem. In our workplaces today, there are many unwritten rules to obey, many superiors and clients to please, and many colleagues to accommodate. These are not necessarily wrong. But when we view work purely as a job, it is natural to first consider our own survival and prospects in our career.

If we choose a profession with this mindset, we will be constantly trying hard to master the art of survival within our field. In Amaziah's eyes, Jeroboam, the king of Israel, was his real boss, and he had to cater to the king's preferences. In today's world, such a mindset is normal. But have we all become like Amaziah in one way or another, heeding the world's beckoning and moving further away from our Creator's call?

The first thing we must examine is our perspectives on work. Most people see work as a way to earn a living or a means for survival. Thus, there is the fear that once it's lost, they will be left with nothing. With this fear comes a more significant problem: idolising work. We feel the drive to earn affirmation from our superiors in order to make our future secure. Work then becomes a tyrant that dictates our lives. We dare not say 'no' to demands at work. As we turn work into an idol to worship, we forget a fundamental fact: life itself is a gift from God. We should rely on God and listen to Him alone.

On the other hand, some people find their work dull and burdensome. They clock in each day just to earn their pay cheque, seeing work as a necessary evil they must endure. As a result, work becomes arduous. They count down the hours until the day's end, longing for the weekend, dreaming of their next holiday, and fixating on the distant promise of retirement.

Viewing work as a means for survival is not necessarily wrong. In fact, God often blesses and provides for us and our loved ones through our jobs. However, problems arise when we elevate our jobs to a position they were never meant to occupy, relying on them to fulfil us in ways only God can. As we let work dictate our lives, we become like Amaziah and deprive our work of the divine purpose God intended.

Work as a gift from God

How does Amos view his work? Let me first introduce a fundamental concept related to work (also mentioned in the chapter on Isaiah) which is rooted in the teachings of creation in Genesis 2, the second account of creation. God cares about our work so deeply that he has already laid down the framework and meaning of work in relation to Him in the creation account. Everything in God's creation is a gift, including work. In Genesis 2:5, we learn about the beginning of creation:

> Now no shrub had yet appeared on the earth and no plant had yet sprung up, for the Lord God had not sent rain on the earth and there was no one to work the ground.

Based on the creation account of plants in Genesis 1–2, plants are the food that God provided for human beings. How was the gift given? It was through rain (provided by God) and cultivation (done by men). God provides for us through the work He gives us.

Earning a living through work is therefore biblical. God indeed provides for us through this gift. Rain and sunlight are certainly provided freely by Him, and even the ability to cultivate and harvest is also given by God so that we may provide for ourselves and enjoy the fruits of it. Ultimately, everything is given by God, but we are called to participate in cultivation and harvest. None of this is to be taken for granted. Having work to do comes entirely by God's grace. We appreciate this truth the most when we experience unemployment or an economic recession. In this sense, it is not inappropriate to see work as a means to make a living, as long as we remember that it is God's gift.

On the other hand, behind every gift is the giver's decision to offer the gift, and more effort on the receiver's part does not necessarily mean more gain. We are not in control. No matter how hard farmers work, the quality of the harvest depends on many factors beyond their control. It is easy for us to forget that everything comes from God because we are accustomed to trying to control every part of the process.

The purpose of work: responding to God's calling

Genesis 1–2 also teaches us another crucial perspective on work that is reflected in Amos's response to Amaziah – work is our response to God's calling. Let's look at 7:14–16:

> **14** Amos answered Amaziah, "I was neither a prophet nor the son of a prophet, but I was a shepherd, and I also took care of sycamore-fig trees. **15** But the Lord took me from tending the flock and said to me, 'Go, prophesy to my people Israel.' **16** Now then, hear the word of the Lord. You say, "Do not prophesy against Israel, and stop preaching against the descendants of Isaac.'"

Amos immediately made it clear that he doesn't see his prophetic work the way Amaziah did. How did he see it? Here's his first line, "I was neither a prophet nor the son of a prophet" (v. 14). Amos meant that he was not the kind of prophet Amaziah had in mind.

At that time, there were schools for prophets, not only among the common people but also within the royal courts. Even kings who did not believe in God would consult prophets before going to war. The court therefore needed a group of royal prophets, trained like government officials, so that they would know how to cater to the king's preferences and speak politically correct 'prophecies'. Such people-pleasing prophets could be found also in the southern kingdom of Judah, such as Hananiah, who opposed Jeremiah (Jeremiah 28:1–17). When enemies attack as part of the Lord's punishment, false prophets would comfort the king, saying, "Don't worry, everything will be fine!"

When Amos said that he was not a prophet, he meant that he was not the kind of vocational prophet who worked under secular values. To Amos, pleasing the king was not the duty of a true prophet.

Amos then explained that he was a shepherd and a tender of sycamore-fig trees. The term 'shepherd' used by Amos here is different from the common term used for other shepherds we know in the Bible such as David, who was also a shepherd. The word here refers to the owner of a pasture, not a worker hired to watch the sheep. He may have many employees, just as wealthy entrepreneurs do today. And a tender of sycamore-fig trees may sound like a gardener, but modern scholars do not think so. Cultivating sycamore-fig trees involves lots of pruning, careful timing and proper management of irrigation. Therefore, in today's terms, Amos was a farm owner and professional horticulturist.

What Amos was actually saying was, "I have two thriving businesses. If I were only interested in advancing my career, I would not be a prophet at all. I have plenty of profit-making opportunities in Judah. So, I'm not the type of prophet you have in mind. I am doing this because it is commanded by the Lord. He told me to leave my home and go speak prophecies to Israel, His people."

Pay special attention to how Amos explained his mission in verse 15:

> "The Lord took me from tending the flock and said to me, 'Go, prophesy to my people Israel.'"

Amos was following a sacred calling, not simply completing a paid job. This was in direct contrast to Amaziah's perspective. Amos's viewpoint meant he didn't need to be concerned about popularity, security or promotion opportunities. His identity and mission were clearly defined by God; they were about God's kingdom and His people. Although the work of the two men looked similar on the surface, their standpoints were completely different. Therefore, the meaning of their work was also completely different.

"I am not . . . , I am . . ."

We can learn from Amos and reflect on our current work or the roles we are playing by using the "I am not . . . , I am . . ." line of thinking. How do you view your work? Do you see it primarily as a means to earn certain rewards or as a sacred calling? How do you react to the 'Amaziahs' in your workplace?

Suppose you are a teacher. What might tempt you to view your work as merely a job? If you view your work as a calling, how would your approach to teaching differ? Some people join the teaching profession simply for a stable work environment. When you teach, are you just fulfilling the requirements of the curriculum or meeting the expectations of parents, or are you fulfilling the calling that God has given you? You can also say, "I am not the kind of teacher who . . . , I am a teacher who . . ." Although the salary and benefits may be the same, different teachers' angles and attitudes can be drastically different.

Those in the insurance industry can also reflect in this way. Are you a salesperson who aims to meet sales targets, or are you a broker who genuinely seeks the best protection for your clients? When you recommend insurance plans to people, is it because God wants you to serve others in this position or because you need to prove yourself to please your supervisor? Do you expand your network to increase your career prospects, or do you do it to fulfil the calling that God has given you? Regardless of the industry you are in, you can reflect in this way by remembering how Amos defined his role and resisted Amaziah.

Another helpful question you can ask yourself is: who do you consider to be your real boss? Amaziah's boss was King Jeroboam of Israel, but Amos's boss was the God who created and called him.

Gifts are the choice of the giver

Calling, like a gift, is not something the recipient can choose. Similarly, Amos had no choice in several matters.

One example is that Amos was to prophesy to the people of Israel on behalf of God (v. 15). The content of the message was not his choice either. Amaziah tried to tell Amos that he could simply prophesy to someone else to avoid trouble. However, where to go and whom to speak to were not choices Amos could make. Doing what needs to be done and speaking what needs to be said requires courage. Sometimes, for comfort or personal gain, we may not want to accept our calling. However, if it is truly a message God wants us to deliver, we cannot remain silent.

Everyone has a calling – a message that God wants you to deliver to others. This message doesn't necessarily have to be spoken; it can be lived out, such as a testimony or a display of certain qualities, character traits, or actions that bless others through you. Living out this calling may require courage and the willingness to stand out in your workplace, showcasing an identity different from the masses in your everyday life. This is your message, and all of it is defined by the Creator.

Apart from the content of the message, Amos's work conditions were also not within his control. Amos had to obey God's command, setting aside his profession as a shepherd and serving as a different kind of shepherd to the people of the northern kingdom. He couldn't bargain for different terms.

We all like to think that we're not the kind of people who would object to or bargain with God if God called us to do something. But here's a question for you: what would your reaction be if a high-earning doctor gave up his medical practice to become a full-time preacher? Many Christians may voice their admiration but secretly think it's a waste of money and talent. However, if that doctor were to give up medicine to take up a billion-dollar business, people would consider it perfectly acceptable. Ultimately, your reaction reveals your values.

This is not to say that being a preacher is more noble or sacred than being a doctor or a businessperson. No, all professions can be sacred and meaningful as long as you are living out God's calling for your life.

Being a slave to a job is never God's calling

In verses 16–17, Amos continued:

> ¹⁶ "Now then, hear the word of the Lord. You say, "Do not prophesy against Israel, and stop preaching against the descendants of Isaac.' ¹⁷ "Therefore this is what the Lord says: "Your wife will become a prostitute in the city, and your sons and daughters will fall by the sword. Your land will be measured and divided up, and you yourself will die in a pagan country. And Israel will surely go into exile, away from their native land.'"

Amos was saying to Amaziah, "You want me to be silent? Now the Lord says this will be your outcome . . ." Amos then specifically prophesied about Amaziah and his family's future (v. 17). The prophecy may seem harsh and inhumane, but it is actually directed at Amaziah's work. In the Law of Moses, priests were not allowed to marry prostitutes (Leviticus 21:7, 14) because the position was sacred. Therefore, when Amos prophesied that Amaziah's wife would become a prostitute, it signified that Amaziah would be stripped of his status as a priest.

Not only would Amaziah's wife and children meet a terrible fate, but his land would "be measured and divided up" and he would "die in a pagan country" (v. 17). The word translated 'pagan' here means 'unclean' or 'impure' in the original Hebrew. Being defiled was something priests dreaded the most. Priests were meant to be the bridge between God and people. Once they were defiled, they could no longer serve as priests. When people sinned, a good priest helped them express repentance to God, reconciled them with God, and prevented them from being punished. But Amaziah had lost the right to hold this sacred position. He had become an incompetent priest and the Israelites suffered greatly as a result.

In other words, Amos was striking back at Amaziah, "You think I will lose my job? You're mistaken. *You* are the one who's losing your job!"

Both Amos and Amaziah had limited choices, but they did have the freedom to choose how they viewed their work and who their true boss was. One had chosen to be a slave to a job; the other had chosen to be a faithful servant of God.

Some Christians think obedience means waiting for God to tell them which profession they should choose. But if God hasn't given you a specific career path, then using your God-given passion and wisdom to make decisions for yourself is also a calling from God. Reflect and examine your heart and attitudes carefully and make a choice in alignment with the interests, abilities and talents that God has given you.

Fulfilling a calling, in simple terms, means that God has called me to do something, and I do my best to do it. Work itself is part of God's calling; thus, doing a job well naturally glorifies God. To glorify means to make goodness visible. In the workplace, you're manifesting God's goodness in a way that others can see. So, if God commissions you to do a job, do it wholeheartedly and live out a good testimony in your position.

VII

What does God want from me?

Knowing your calling through knowing God deeper

13

Abram (Abraham)

In this section, we shift our focus to two other pivotal figures in the Old Testament whose lives offer us invaluable insights into the concept of calling. Let us first consider Abraham.

Christians love retelling the story of Abraham, our faith hero, as a role model for great faith and courage. However, we often forget one fact: in the famous chapter of Genesis 12, God didn't call Abraham; He called Abram, the one who struggled in faith and slowly grew in his faith journey in baby steps. God called Abram when he was still Abram, and it was God who gradually shaped and transformed him into the Abraham we admire today. His journey started when God reached out to him in Genesis 12:1–3:

> [1] The Lord had said to Abram, "Go from your country, your people and your father's household to the land I will show you. [2] "I will make you into a great nation, and I will bless you; I will make your name great, and you will be a blessing. [3] I will bless those who bless you, and whoever curses you I will curse; and all peoples on earth will be blessed through you."

The story of Abram obeying God's calling has been frequently featured in numerous Christian books and Sunday School lessons. In the beginning of the story, God instructed Abram to leave three things behind: his country, his people, and his father's household. "Country" refers to the place where he resided, which was Harran. He had to leave his hometown and go to an unknown land. His "people" refers to his family, his whole clan. He had to separate himself from his relatives. "His father's household" refers to his inheritance; he had to abandon all the possessions left to him by his father.

The essence of calling: letting go before receiving

This was not an easy task. If you leave your dwelling place, depart from your loved ones, and forsake all your belongings, you're being completely uprooted. God was asking Abram to forsake everything and start a new life in another world. In return, God made him a promise corresponding to what he had surrendered: he would become a great nation.

Throughout the Bible, calling and promise are closely connected. Promises, in this context, chiefly pertain to spiritual blessings, such as enjoying a deep relationship with God. A divine calling typically demands that you must let go of everything you have relied on. This is difficult, and many people are unwilling to obey. However, a calling often demands that we do so.

How did Abram respond? Let's turn to verses 4 and 5:

> [4] So Abram went, as the Lord had told him; and Lot went with him. Abram was seventy-five years old when he set out from Harran. [5] He took his wife Sarai, his nephew Lot, all the possessions they had accumulated and the people they had acquired in Harran, and they set out for the land of Canaan, and they arrived there.

Abram appears to have obeyed without hesitation. However, did you notice he didn't *fully* obey? God commanded him to leave all his relatives, but he brought his nephew Lot along. He also took with him the possessions and servants he had acquired in Harran. Abram wasn't as obedient or confident as we imagine, at least not in the beginning. He didn't leave everything behind and set off with the carefree attitude that many children's Sunday

School materials like to portray. No, he took many of his family members, servants and possessions with him. He actually only obeyed one-third of what God commanded him: to leave Harran.

The faith hero who was not yet a faith hero

Abraham, the renowned Father of Faith, didn't become a faith hero all at once, but one step at a time.

Why didn't Abram fully obey? From a human perspective, this is understandable. First, he and his wife Sarai were still childless, which was a matter of great concern for him. He might have regarded Lot as a relative who could carry on his lineage. Second, travelling through the wilderness in those days wasn't as convenient as it is today. Survival required taking along livestock. Servants were necessary too, since all those possessions and livestock needed to be taken care of throughout the journey. Abram was a wealthy man, and his willingness to leave his homeland was commendable. Perhaps that was the level of obedience he could cope with at that time.

In other words, God's calling to Abram unfolded slowly, step by step. Abram's faith might not have been great in the beginning. He was simply responding to God's calling based on what he could handle and the circumstances he could perceive at that time. The limitations he was facing were great; God had disclosed only very limited information. He had no guarantees or resources, and such challenges are not a joke.

Our response to God's calling often follows a familiar pattern – we yearn for a complete understanding of every part of the plan before we dare to take the first step. Insecurity and uncertainty hold us back from wholeheartedly obeying God's calling. The fear of leaving our comfort zone, our safe haven, is the most typical obstacle. We fear taking risks when there's no clarity, no assurance of resources, and little knowledge of our destination. This could be a real test of faith.

Therefore, Abram's journey to become the Father of Faith was in fact a long journey in which he slowly learned to trust, stumbling along the way. However, he possessed a remarkable virtue – the willingness to step out even when he had no clue where he was going. That is the lesson we need to learn: we don't need to know all of God's plans right away, nor do we need to calculate all the details. We just need to take one step at a time towards where God wants us to go.

Finding one's calling takes one step at a time

As soon as Abram set out, he encountered all sorts of problems. The first was the Canaanites who were already living in the land. Then there was the second trouble. Let's read verses 10 to 20:

> 10 Now there was a famine in the land, and Abram went down to Egypt to live there for a while because the famine was severe. 11 As he was about to enter Egypt, he said to his wife Sarai, "I know what a beautiful woman you are. 12 When the Egyptians see you, they will say, 'This is his wife.' Then they will kill me but will let you live. 13 Say you are my sister, so that I will be treated well for your sake and my life will be spared because of you."
>
> 14 When Abram came to Egypt, the Egyptians saw that Sarai was a very beautiful woman. 15 And when Pharaoh's officials saw her, they praised her to Pharaoh, and she was taken into his palace. 16 He treated Abram well for her sake, and Abram acquired sheep and cattle, male and female donkeys, male and female servants, and camels. 17 But the Lord inflicted serious diseases on Pharaoh and his household because of Abram's wife Sarai. 18 So Pharaoh summoned Abram. "What have you done to me?" he said. "Why didn't you tell me she was your wife? 19 Why did you say, 'She is my sister,' so that I took her to be my wife? Now then, here is your wife. Take her and go!" 20 Then Pharaoh gave orders about Abram to his men, and they sent him on his way, with his wife and everything he had.

First, the land that God has given him was struck by famine. This isn't how we usually picture God's calling. Abram left with many possessions, but a horrible famine caused the death of his cattle and sheep, leaving him with nothing. God compelled him to flee to Egypt where he learned to let go completely and then later bestowed everything upon him once again. Only God remained as his reliable support.

Abram was constantly on the verge of getting into trouble. Initially, he reacted to crises much like any ordinary person would: he relied on his own instincts for survival, incorporating his own reasoning and human factors into God's calling. He told Pharaoh that his wife Sarai was his sister (Genesis 12:10-20), which could have had severe consequences. God had not yet promised Abram a son who would be the blessing to all nations. However, if Pharaoh had truly taken Sarai as his wife, then Abram would have jeopardised the future descendants that God had in store for him. Thankfully, God intervened and protected them, and Pharaoh realised the truth in time, thus preventing a disaster.

Many scholars have tried to defend Abram's choice of action, pointing out that there was a custom of calling one's wife "sister" in the neighbouring countries at that time. Abram might not have been lying. However, this custom didn't apply in Egypt. Pharaoh, seeing Sarai's beauty, bestowed many riches upon Abram. Later, when the truth was revealed, Abram left with those riches. God returned to Abram all the possessions He had told him to let go of.

As a result, Abram now possessed more than what God had initially asked him to give up. Abram originally had expected to rely on himself and his own resources for greater assurance, but God had a valuable lesson for him to learn. Like Abram, our vision is very limited, and we often think that we need to possess certain things to feel secure. But God doesn't consider these things necessary. His desire is for us to let go of these attachments first, to embark on the journey empty-handed, and then He will supply us through His means, making sure we lack nothing.

This doesn't mean that Abram had done the right thing. God has a way of turning things around, though, transforming human weakness into paths of blessings. The Bible never promises that responding to God's calling will be obstacle-free. We must be careful not to let these difficulties hinder us from obeying God. Abram's foolish act showed he was not yet truly following God's lead.

Gradually, Abram grew in his understanding of and obedience to God's guidance. He searched and wandered in circles, and slowly became wiser and more discerning. To avoid further trouble, he allowed his nephew Lot to choose the land first (Genesis 13). Lot opted for the lush, fertile land east of the Jordan River. Then Abram headed west, towards the promised land designated by God.

This is how God led Abram as he slowly discovered his true home. Along the way, he faced many challenges and tests, but he was able to recognise God's guiding hand more and more. When we respond to our calling, we also encounter obstacles. The challenge lies in not being able to see the whole picture in advance. We must, however, refrain from solving problems in our own way – which only complicates matters further – but follow God's leading.

This chapter in Genesis shows us that responding to our calling involves many struggles and learning experiences. As we continue step by step, our calling becomes clearer. God delights in leading us according to His purpose and teaching us to recognise His hand.

The ultimate test: let go of your son

Genesis 15–16 explores Abram's primary concern – securing a rightful heir. With Lot gone, who would be his heir? Given his advanced age, this problem loomed large. Only his servant, Eliezer, remained as a possible heir, and Abram initially thought he would be the one (Genesis 15:2). Later, when Hagar, the maidservant, gave birth to Ishmael (Genesis 16), Abram assumed Ishmael was the one promised by God.

We tend to expect God to accomplish His promises in ways that make sense to us. At that time, it was customary for childless men to pass their inheritance to their male servants or to have children through concubines. This solution seemed natural for Abram. However, God had different plans.

We need to be cautious and avoid attempting to engineer our way out of our problems by our own understanding and efforts. Despite the apparent impossibility of Abram fathering a child at the age of ninety-nine, God continually stretched the boundaries of his trust until Abram ultimately became Abraham (Genesis 17:5).

Finally, Isaac was born to Abraham and Sarah (chapter 21). Now we fast forward to Genesis 22, which presents God's greatest, ultimate test for Abraham – the sacrifice of his son Isaac:

> [1] Some time later God tested Abraham. He said to him, "Abraham!"
> "Here I am," he replied.
> [2] Then God said, "Take your son, your only son, whom you love – Isaac – and go to the region of Moriah. Sacrifice him there as a burnt offering on a mountain that I will show you."
> [3] Early the next morning Abraham got up and loaded his donkey. He took with him two of his servants and his son Isaac. When he had cut enough wood for the burnt offering, he set out for the place God had told him about.

Notice the passage begins by clearly stating that God was testing Abraham. What was being tested? At first glance, it might appear to be solely his faith, but it went beyond that; it was a test of Abraham's love as well. God emphasizes that Isaac is "your only son, whom you love". God wanted Abraham to go through this trial to know that his true blessings were in God, not in Isaac.

Just as when God first commanded Abraham to leave his homeland, this time he also didn't know exactly where he was going. God mentioned the name Moriah, but Moriah being a vast piece of land, Abraham had no knowledge of the specific mountain he should journey toward. Nevertheless, he embarked on the journey. It was only on the third day that he "saw the place in the distance" (v. 4). He saw the destination only after arriving in the area.

This is the lesson we need to learn: when God calls, take the first step.

In the case of Abraham, it was particularly challenging because he didn't know where he was supposed to go, and even more bewildering, he didn't understand why he was being asked to sacrifice his own son, Isaac. Wasn't Isaac the promised descendant? Why would God ask him to kill Isaac now?

This was beyond human comprehension and capacity, but despite the confusion, Abraham chose to embark on his journey without knowing the details, much like when he left Harran. What sets Abraham apart is his willingness to take the first step. As it was previously mentioned, "So Abram went, as the LORD had told him" (Genesis 12:4), and now we see again, "Early the next morning, Abraham got up and set out for the place God had told him about" (22:3). Let's continue with verses 5–8:

> ⁵ He said to his servants, "Stay here with the donkey while I and the boy go over there. We will worship and then we will come back to you."
>
> ⁶ Abraham took the wood for the burnt offering and placed it on his son Isaac, and he himself carried the fire and the knife. As the two of them went on together, ⁷ Isaac spoke up and said to his father Abraham, "Father?"
>
> "Yes, my son?" Abraham replied.
>
> "The fire and wood are here," Isaac said, "but where is the lamb for the burnt offering?"
>
> ⁸ Abraham answered, "God himself will provide the lamb for the burnt offering, my son." And the two of them went on together.

The verb 'go' in Abraham's instructions (v. 5) and in the description of how the father and son "went on together" (v. 6) are the same word. They belong to the same root as the previous two instances when Abraham went out according to God's command. This time, Abraham left all his servants behind and took only what he needed for the sacrifice: wood and a knife. Verse 3 states that he had prepared the wood for the burnt offering before leaving home. He had prepared everything needed to obey God's command and then journeyed toward the destination together with his son.

Jehovah Jireh: The Lord provides (and sees!)

Scripture doesn't describe Abraham's feelings, but we can imagine that he must have had a horrible night, with his mind exploding with anxiety and questions. Yet he still did everything he was commanded.

Isaac noticed that everything for the sacrifice was there except a lamb. Among the three patriarchs, Abraham, Isaac, and Jacob, Isaac is the least mentioned figure in the Bible. Some people even say that Isaac's only significant contribution in the Bible was to prompt his father to make the profound statement: "God himself will provide the lamb for the burnt offering" (22:8).

Interestingly, the verb 'provide' in the original text also means "to see". In fact, there are many instances of 'seeing' in this passage. First, Abraham had to venture out before he could see. Now Isaac said that he could not see the lamb, and in his reply to his son Abraham was essentially saying, "I cannot see it either, but God can see it." It doesn't matter if I can't see. God can see and that's enough.

There was a story about a blind little girl playing on her father's knee, and her cousin wanted to play a prank on her, so he quietly picked her up and ran, hoping to scare her. But the little girl didn't scream; she wasn't afraid at all. The cousin asked, "Why aren't you afraid?" The girl said, "I can't see, but Daddy can see. Since Daddy didn't stop you, then it must be okay." Faith is just like this. God knows what He is doing. He will closely watch over everything. Our calling may be incomprehensible to us, but it doesn't matter because the God who calls us sees everything.

Genesis 22:9–14:

> 9 When they reached the place God had told him about, Abraham built an altar there and arranged the wood on it. He bound his son Isaac and laid him on the altar, on top of the wood. 10 Then he reached out his hand and took the knife to slay his son. 11 But the angel of the Lord called out to him from heaven, "Abraham!

Abraham!"

"Here I am," he replied. [12] "Do not lay a hand on the boy," he said. "Do not do anything to him. Now I know that you fear God, because you have not withheld from me your son, your only son."

[13] Abraham looked up and there in a thicket he saw a ram caught by its horns. He went over and took the ram and sacrificed it as a burnt offering instead of his son.

[14] So Abraham called that place The Lord Will Provide. And to this day it is said, "On the mountain of the Lord it will be provided."

God commanded Abraham to offer Isaac as a burnt offering (v. 2), and Abraham obeyed literally, binding his beloved son and placing him on the altar, ready to kill him. If it were you, could you do it? Abraham could. According to the book of Hebrews, Abraham trusted God to such an extent that he believed that God could raise people from the dead (Hebrews 11:19). He believed that even if he killed his son, God could still resurrect his son. His faith and hope in God enabled him to obey God, but what is primarily emphasised here is his love for God. He loved God more than he loved his own son.

Had Abraham obeyed without any struggle or doubt? He probably had a sleepless night, spent tossing and turning. But Scripture tells us he set out with Isaac early the next day, along with the prepared wood and knife.

In any case, asking a father to sacrifice his son is unimaginably unreasonable. God's request seemed absurd and barbarous. This passage has prompted at least two difficult questions. One, how could God make such a request? Two, if God really wanted to test Abraham, why did He provide an animal as a substitute? The angel of the Lord could have simply said, "Don't harm your son" and ended the story. Wouldn't that have been sufficient? Why did an animal have to die?

God's calling goes beyond what we can see

The author of Genesis hints at the answer. The passage not only makes it clear that Abraham offered that ram "instead of his son" (v. 13) as a burnt offering, but also includes another crucial hint – Moriah. Moriah is the name of a mountain located in Jerusalem, where according to the Books of Chronicles Solomon built the temple. David wanted to build a temple for God, but God said that it should be built by his son Solomon. Before David passed away, he made all the preparations, and the chosen location was Mount Moriah. So, we know that this location would later be the site of the Lord's temple where sacrifices were to be made for God's people. This ram represented not only Isaac, but also the Lamb of God who will be sacrificed for the world.

While it might seem that God gave Abraham a ridiculous command, Scripture tells us that what God asked of Abraham was exactly what He Himself chose to do. Isaac was Abraham's cherished son; God sacrificed His own begotten Son to die in place of all humanity. This is incomprehensible, but such is God's love for us. God made the ultimate sacrifice, giving up His Son for the world. This is the most profound expression of love God has given to the world. It's challenging for us to grasp, as such love is beyond our understanding.

The love demonstrated by Jesus on the cross is inexplicable. God has prepared everything for us, even the perfect salvation plan for the world, allowing us to step forward confidently to receive His calling for our lives. Of course, it wasn't possible for Abraham to comprehend the full implication of these events at the time. He could hardly understand the foreshadowing significance of God providing the ram at Mount Moriah. Yet, despite his limited understanding, Abraham obeyed and made the first step. What about us? Today, with the full Old and New Testaments at our fingertips, what we can see is much more than what Abraham could see. We, who know the meaning of Jehovah Jireh, can confidently obey and trust the One who calls us.

14

Joseph

Another biblical character who faced the test of learning about God's calling is Joseph. Joseph's life was filled with hardships. From a young age, he was sold by his brothers to traders who took him to Egypt to work as a slave. Despite his circumstances, he excelled as a slave and was promoted by his master. However, he was unjustly accused by his master's wife when he resisted her advances and was incarcerated. In prison, he interpreted dreams for Pharaoh's chief cupbearer, who was later released but forgot about him, leaving him abandoned in prison for two long years. In short, his journey was 'a series of unfortunate events'.

What can we learn about God's calling from Joseph's experiences? According to the Bible, Joseph accomplished at least two great things in adversity. First, he remained steadfast and never gave up. Second, he held onto his identity in God and never indulged in sinful desires.

The call to persevere and remain faithful

Let's be honest. Many Christians, when facing similar circumstances, would become resentful, filled with anger, and question why God allowed such things to happen to them. Challenges in life can easily lead to frustration and demoralisation. But Joseph didn't show any signs of compromising. He did his best to live up to his identity in God, never giving up. The Bible tells us that in everything Joseph did, God was with him (Genesis 39:2–5, 21–23).

Through his perseverance and integrity, he rose to the esteemed position of steward in the house of an Egyptian official. But he faced a moral dilemma when his master's wife tried to seduce him. Yielding to her advances might have offered him a chance to elevate his status even further. Yet, Joseph, in his steadfast commitment to righteousness, rebuffed her firmly:

> **8** But he refused. "With me in charge," he told her, "my master does not concern himself with anything in the house; everything he owns he has entrusted to my care. **9** No-one is greater in this house than I am. My master has withheld nothing from me except you, because you are his wife. How then could I do such a wicked thing and sin against God?" (Genesis 39:8–9)

His resolve was rooted not in self-preservation, but in his devotion to God and a profound sense of purity and dignity.

Difficult circumstances have a way of shaking our core values. Some might reason, "Since God treats me this way, and since I'm so miserable, why shouldn't I do as I please?" Christians are not immune to this temptation, with many finding solace in indulgence and defiance against God. But Joseph's example stands out. Faced with such dilemmas, he asked, "How can I commit this sin and betray God?" Never wavering in the face of adversities, Joseph clung to his integrity. He refused to belittle or indulge himself.

The verb 'do' in Joseph's response (v. 9) is the same word used earlier in verse 3, where it says, "The Lord was with him and . . . gave him success in everything he did." Joseph couldn't see God's future plan for his life or why he had to go through such hardships and betrayals. At this moment, Joseph wasn't aware of God's grand design for his life or the reason behind his ordeals. We, with hindsight, understand these tribulations paved the way to his future accomplishments and leadership. But Joseph, during his trials, had no such foresight. He didn't need to know all the answers; he only needed to know that God is faithful and trustworthy. Though unaware of the bigger picture, he remained faithful without allowing his circumstances to dictate his reactions.

Following God's calling doesn't mean finding out exactly what God has planned, but it means diligently living out the life God has given us today and remaining faithful to Him in His presence. Joseph's experiences teach us two precious lessons:

1. Even without much knowledge of God's bigger plans, he persisted in doing what was right in God's eyes. Our vision is often narrow and limited, so we shouldn't let it dictate our choices.
2. Joseph's actions always mirrored his profound bond with God, ensuring he never stooped below his dignity. We, too, bear the same cherished identity in God, and no hardship should ever prompt us to sin against God.

Joseph held onto these principles throughout, and God granted him abundant grace to triumph in difficult times.

Calling is not only about the future but also the past

In addition to his perseverance, Joseph had spiritual insight. He recognised God's grace amidst the bitterness of his experiences. Many of us are familiar with the story of the emotional reunion between Joseph and his older brothers, younger brother Benjamin, and father Jacob (Genesis 45). Before jumping to the happy ending, I'd like to first focus on passages that shed light on the key to Joseph's spiritual strength. In Genesis 41, Joseph finally emerged from his bitter situation, becoming the second-in-command in Egypt (41:43), and even starting a family. The names he gave his two sons reflected his perspectives:

> Joseph named his firstborn Manasseh and said, "It is because God has made me forget all my trouble and all my father's household."

> **52** The second son he named Ephraim and said, "It is because God has made me fruitful in the land of my suffering." (Genesis 41:51–52)

The name Manasseh means "making to forget", signifying forgetting all troubles and remembering only grace. Forgetting doesn't mean erasing memories or deliberately avoiding thoughts about them. In fact, it's impossible to forget such painful experiences. Joseph's idea of forgetting was not denying the past, but letting grace replace those painful experiences so that whenever his memory was prompted by past people or events, he would remember how immense God's grace was.

This mindset can be likened to that of a woman in labour. Jesus used this example when bidding farewell to His disciples: "A woman giving birth to a child has pain because her time has come; but when her baby is born, she forgets the anguish because of her joy that a child is born into the world" (John 16:21). The pain of childbirth is severe, but once the child is born, the woman no longer holds onto the pain. This doesn't mean she forgets the excruciating pain she went through; rather, her pain has been replaced by something treasurable, beautiful, and precious.

Joseph's perspective was similar. He recognised God's grace in the midst of the bitter experiences. He didn't resent the past or carry grudges; instead, he saw himself as highly blessed, understanding that God hadn't mistreated him in the slightest. Indeed, each step in his journey had its purpose, and now he could finally see that it was all God's grace.

The name he gave to his other son – Ephraim – also carried great significance (Genesis 41:52). The name means "fruitfulness" or "abundance". Joseph recognised that his fruitfulness in the land of suffering was God's amazing work. God not only replaced his troubles with grace, but grace also triumphed over his afflictions. What had once been extremely painful now became incredibly sweet, bearing abundant fruit. Joseph saw how his troubles had been immensely useful, and they no longer bothered him.

The names of the two sons revealed the infinite gratitude in Joseph's heart. Joseph had been subjected to unfair treatment and painful trauma throughout his life. Although the unfortunate events couldn't be erased, he reconciled with his past without holding any grudges but filling his heart with praise. He saw himself as immensely blessed, recognising how God's grace overshadows all the bitterness. This empowered him to eventually reconcile with his brothers, truly forgiving them.

Reinterpreting the past: Sent, not sold

Genesis 45:4–13 records the words of Joseph to his brothers in their reunion. Verses 4 to 8 are particularly well-known as Joseph acknowledged God as the mastermind behind the whole story:

> **4** Then Joseph said to his brothers, "Come close to me." When they had done so, he said, "I am your brother Joseph, the one you sold into Egypt! **5** And now, do not be distressed and do not be angry with yourselves for selling me here, because it was to save lives that God sent me ahead of you. **6** For two years now there has been famine in the land, and for the next five years there will be no ploughing and reaping. **7** But God sent me ahead of you to preserve for you a remnant on earth and to save your lives by a great deliverance. **8** So then, it was not you who sent me here, but God. He made me father to Pharaoh, lord of his entire household and ruler of all Egypt."

When Joseph revealed his identity to his brothers, his words were similar to those of Amos when he resisted a false prophet who was trying to question his approach to his prophetic career. Yet Joseph spoke not of his work, but of his personal experience. Amos said, "I was neither a prophet nor the son of a prophet…but the Lord took me from tending the flock and said to me, 'Go, prophesy to my people Israel.'" (Amos 7: 14-15) Amos was essentially saying, "I'm a prophet sent by God Himself." Joseph also said, "I am not sold; I was sent by God." If you were Joseph, perhaps you would want to remind the brothers of all the things you had suffered. Instead, he said, "I am sent by God." The suffering he endured due to human errors in the past had now been transformed into blessings from God. When Joseph asserted that he was sent by God instead of being sold by his brothers, he was signifying a notion of 'authorisation'. The act of sending someone to accomplish a purpose is essentially authorising that person to do the work on your behalf. Our understanding of calling should be the same: "I am God's authorised representative, sent on a mission. God places me in this position. He delivers me and protects me."

This is not to say that Joseph condoned sin or accepted his brothers' wrongdoing. Rather, he saw the entire situation from God's perspective and understood how God uses human failures to achieve something far greater. Joseph must have reconciled with his past before he could reconcile with his brothers; otherwise, his heart would have been filled with bitterness, making it difficult for him to continue to the next phase of the journey God had prepared for him.

God's calling embraces the reinterpretation of our own lives. Do we also carry many regrets and unresolved traumas from our past? Consider this statement: "I am not . . . , I am . . .". We can also reflect along this line and allow God to transform our thoughts, revealing His hidden grace and grand, overarching plan.

While Amos spoke about the proper attitudes towards work, emphasising that God is our true boss, Joseph spoke about life, stating that everything that happens is from God, the mastermind behind our entire lives. Joseph's words testified that it was not his brothers who made him who he was; it was God who led him all the way, preparing, protecting, and blessing him.

Great blessings, great missions

Genesis 49 records the blessings Joseph's father Jacob gave to each of his sons before his death. When it was Joseph's turn to receive his blessings, Jacob said,

> Joseph is a fruitful vine,
>> a fruitful vine near a spring,
>> whose branches climb over a wall. (Genesis 49:22)

"Fruitful vine" is actually the name God gave to Joseph through Jacob's blessing.

What's special about a fruitful vine? While a tree may have numerous branches, the branch representing Joseph yielded abundant fruit. Yet, Jacob's description doesn't focus on the quantity of fruit on this branch or make comparisons with other branches. Instead, he emphasizes the exceptional length of this particular branch, noting that it even extends over a wall.

Let's consider this: imagine you're a tree with numerous branches, all growing lushly. Among them, one branch bears an exceptionally large number of fruit. This branch represents Joseph, and his name indeed means "increase" or "add more". The more fruit he bore, the larger the space the branch needed. Therefore, God allowed Joseph to extend beyond the wall, far to Egypt. However, stretching out is not always a good thing. As the saying goes, "A tall tree catches the wind", and Joseph initially experienced a series of storms and hardships.

But what did Jacob say next? In verses 23 to 26:

> ²³ With bitterness archers attacked him;
>> they shot at him with hostility.
> ²⁴ But his bow remained steady,
>> his strong arms stayed limber,
>> because of the hand of the Mighty One of Jacob,
>> because of the Shepherd, the Rock of Israel,
> ²⁵ because of your father's God, who helps you,
>> because of the Almighty, who blesses you
>> with blessings of the skies above,
>> blessings of the deep springs below,

> blessings of the breast and womb.
> **26** Your father's blessings are greater
>   than the blessings of the ancient mountains,
>   than the bounty of the age-old hills.
>   Let all these rest on the head of Joseph,
>   on the brow of the prince among his brothers.

Jacob's message was significant: if you want more blessings and bear more fruit, you will face more challenges, but your "bow [will remain] steady" (v. 24), meaning you don't have to fear these challenges. God will grant you strength and stability, and as long as you do what you ought to do and refrain from what you shouldn't do, God will handle the rest.

Here, Jacob referred to God in three distinct ways: "the Shepherd, the Rock of Israel", "the Mighty One of Jacob" and "your father's God". All three essentially related to Jacob himself, and each of these descriptions highlighted a different aspect of God's character.

The first is "the Shepherd, the Rock of Israel", illustrating protection. A shepherd protects the sheep, preventing them from predators' attack. A rock is sturdy, providing shelter and security. This symbolises God's strong and reliable care. The second title "the Mighty One of Jacob" depicts a warrior. This signified that God would surely help Joseph overcome all attacks and difficulties. The third, "your father's God", denotes not only God's sovereignty but also belongingness to God. This was Joseph's most solid guarantee.

Joseph's blessings are the greatest among his brothers. "Blessings of the skies above, blessings of the deep springs below, blessings of the breast and womb" (v. 25) all belonged to him, meaning that such blessings extended to the next generation, and even to all future generations; this likely refers to how God saved the entire Israelite nation through Joseph's experiences.

Joseph inherited the most blessed name. His life might have been tumultuous, but he remained steadfast to his calling, and he had nothing to fear. Therefore, as God has called us to live a blessed, abundant life, we need not tirelessly chase after blessings for ourselves, nor should we dread the obstacles that may arise. Like Joseph, we aren't in control of all the trials and challenges that cross our paths. The crux is how we respond. We can succumb to despair, eventually messing up everything; or we can hold onto God as Joseph did, and ultimately triumph over trials with God's grace.

VIII

Is the Lord calling you? (Part 1)

An ordinary life called by an extraordinary God

15

Moses

To many Christians, the concept of 'God's calling' seems abstract and elusive. We long to discern what God specifically wants in our lives. Some Christians even try look for special signs from heaven. However, the Bible doesn't always provide the clear-cut instructions many of us wish for.

As we study the Bible, however, we can make a couple of helpful observations. One is that whenever God gave an important message or instructions to people, it always happened when they were doing what they would normally be doing on an ordinary day, when they weren't expecting to hear from God. Shepherds were shepherding, fishermen were fishing, and priests were carrying out their routine duties. Another observation is that the people who were meant to hear God's message never had a problem understanding the message. There was no need for them to say a special prayer or decipher a secret code. God never expects anyone to be Sherlock Holmes or Indiana Jones to get His messages. When the time is right, God communicates directly and clearly, and He means exactly what He says. Are we surprised?

In this and the following section, we will explore how God's glory is unveiled in His calling of the ordinary. Let's begin with Moses' story. Many Christians are familiar with the story of how God called Moses in the famous burning bush encounter. While only two verses (Exodus 3:2-3) describe the burning bush, a total of 36 verses (3:4-4:17) are devoted to record the extensive dialogue between God and Moses. This extensive coverage reflects the fact that a divine calling is not about a 'sign', but an ongoing process of knowing God. Here's how the story began (Exodus 3:1–6):

> [1] Now Moses was tending the flock of Jethro his father-in-law, the priest of Midian, and he led the flock to the far side of the wilderness and came to Horeb, the mountain of God. [2] There the angel of the Lord appeared to him in flames of fire from within a bush. Moses saw that though the bush was on fire it did not burn up. [3] So Moses thought, "I will go over and see this strange sight – why the bush does not burn up."
>
> [4] When the Lord saw that he had gone over to look, God called to him from within the bush, "Moses! Moses!"
>
> And Moses said, "Here I am."
>
> [5] "Do not come any closer," God said. "Take off your sandals, for the place where you are standing is holy ground." [6] Then he said, "I am the God of your father, the God of Abraham, the God of Isaac and the God of Jacob." At this, Moses hid his face, because he was afraid to look at God.

It is not about the burning bush

I have heard many Christians ask, "Will God call me? I haven't seen my burning bush yet." We think if we could only have a great vision like Moses had, then everything in our lives would become clear. However, what Moses saw in this incident was actually quite limited. A bush that is burning doesn't convey much. The one and only purpose of this vision was simply to attract Moses's attention. Furthermore, the bush itself didn't help Moses understand his calling at all, and what Moses really needed in his calling – obedience and God's faithfulness – had nothing to do with the burning bush. The focal point of the story lies not in the peculiar vision of the bush, but in the setting and God's Word.

What kind of setting was Moses in when God called him? The passage provides a clear picture of it. It took place in the wilderness, which was simply where Moses was tending to his father-in-law's sheep. The desert was his everyday workplace. God's calling often occurs in the most ordinary circumstances, in our day-to-day workplaces or in our personal lives.

Pay attention to God's command for Moses not to approach the bush. God said,

> "Do not come any closer . . . Take off your sandals, for the place where you are standing is holy ground." (v. 5)

Removing his sandals signified not only respect but it also carried a deeper meaning. In the cultural context of that time, only the master of a household wore shoes; servants and maids did not wear them. Shoes were a symbol of social status. God was declaring, "This is my territory. I am the master, and everything is under my authority."

When God calls us, the first thing He wants us to understand is, "This is my domain, not yours."

God then reminded Moses of their relationship (v. 6):

> "I am the God of your father, the God of Abraham, the God of Isaac and the God of Jacob."

God declared that Moses's entire family heritage, his roots and identity all belonged to Him. The same is true for us today. Everything we have, our entire existence, belongs to Him alone. Every facet of our lives, whether it's work, family, ministry, or relationships, is solely under God's authority. In fact, our entire lives are sacred ground to God, and His calling encompasses every area. There is no division between sacred and secular callings. All callings are sacred because of who we are in God.

Therefore, God's calling doesn't necessarily involve grand visions or miraculous signs. Visions don't help us understand our real calling. God's

Word does. What we really need is the confirmation of our true identity and our relationship with God. We must first acknowledge that we belong only to God. This is what the young Levite (see Chapter 9 of this book) failed to understand.

The essence of calling: what's in God's heart

Let's continue with verses 7–10:

> ⁷ The Lord said, "I have indeed seen the misery of my people in Egypt. I have heard them crying out because of their slave drivers, and I am concerned about their suffering. ⁸ So I have come down to rescue them from the hand of the Egyptians and to bring them up out of that land into a good and spacious land, a land flowing with milk and honey – the home of the Canaanites, Hittites, Amorites, Perizzites, Hivites and Jebusites. ⁹ And now the cry of the Israelites has reached me, and I have seen the way the Egyptians are oppressing them. ¹⁰ So now, go. I am sending you to Pharaoh to bring my people the Israelites out of Egypt."

God calls when He sees a need – His people were suffering horribly under oppression and in desperate need of rescue. What stands out in these verses is the extensive description of God's concern for the Israelites. Only at the end is the actual instruction revealed (v. 10). The text doesn't mention what Moses saw when he approaches the bush, but it meticulously highlights what God was seeing. We may yearn for visions and special signs, but Scripture shows us that what really matters is what God sees.

A calling is a burden; it is seeing a need – not from a human perspective, but from God's perspective. Moses had long witnessed the plight of the Israelites, stored it in his heart, and was eager to save his compatriots from their suffering. However, his initial efforts failed, forcing him to flee (Exodus 2). Now God wanted him to know, "It's not what you see, it's what I see. I have long seen the distress of the Israelites, and now I will deliver them."

A calling revolves around God; Moses is not the protagonist – God is. God knows His people's needs and delivers. Therefore, a calling is never about what "I" can do or what "I" see; it centres around God and what He sees. When we contemplate our calling, we often only think about ourselves: what am I to do? Am I capable? Did I hear God correctly? Am I going in the right direction? Everything revolves around our own concerns. However, Scripture challenges this mindset and directs us to look at calling from God's standpoint – to understand that it's not about us at all.

The timing of the calling

God's calling is often intertwined with the needs of the time. The passage shows us the circumstances in which Moses was called, reflecting the suffering of the people God cared about. When God calls someone to serve Him, it signifies His readiness to act and show His grace.

When God calls us, we are essentially extending God's grace to others. Many believers are afraid of hearing God's calling, afraid it will bring great hardship, believing they will suffer losses. We must abandon this mindset. From God's perspective, a calling is not an arduous task; it is a gracious God showing His people compassion and favour. We should rejoice and be glad when we hear God calling us!

Therefore, a calling is not a heavy burden. If today God calls you, stirs a certain passion or burden within you, and asks you to meet certain needs in this world, it is because He has decided to extend grace and take action. He is commissioning you to partner with Him. It is all about Him and His purpose.

Calling as a precious gift

From this perspective, a calling can also be seen as a precious gift God gives for the world. For hundreds of years, the Israelites endured oppression, and Moses was the most precious gift God could have given to His people at that time in history. When Moses was born, he was the only surviving male among the Israelites. He was specially set apart by God for a special purpose. Everyone else in the Israelite community was illiterate with no chance of going to school. Moses, however, grew up in the Egyptian palace, receiving the best education in the most advanced civilisation in the world at the time.

> "Moses was educated in all the wisdom of the Egyptians and was powerful in speech and action." (Acts 7:22)

He was the one who would write the entire Law of Moses, after all! With the unparalleled opportunities he was given, he could have easily forgotten about his heritage and distanced himself from his people. But he felt a deep connection to his fellow Israelites and was unable to turn a blind eye to their suffering.

God spared Moses's life and bestowed His favour upon him. From the very beginning, it was God's plan and work. Looking back, do you see how God has been preparing you? He has given you specific opportunities and experiences that others may not have in order to equip you and make you a gift. God *never* asked Moses (or anyone else) to do a spiritual gifts test to help him discover his gifts. Moses *was* the gift. God had been slowly preparing and shaping Moses for 80 years so that he would be the perfect gift to His people.

We are the gifts that God has prepared long ago, and He will send us out at the appropriate time to be given to those in need. This beautiful concept is also found elsewhere in the Bible. In Ephesians 4:11–12, we read about the gifts of apostles, prophets, evangelists, pastors, and teachers, but the emphasis here is not on the specific abilities themselves but on the fact that God gives these *people* to the church "to equip his people for works of service". Christians who wonder if they have the right gifts to serve God are asking the wrong question. The gifts do come from God, but the Scripture reminds us that that we ourselves can be the gifts prepared by God.

It's never about 'me'

Unfortunately, Moses kept thinking about himself. Exodus 3: 11–12 tell us:

> [11] But Moses said to God, "Who am I that I should go to Pharaoh and bring the Israelites out of Egypt?"
>
> [12] And God said, "I will be with you. And this will be the sign to you that it is I who have sent you: when you have brought the people out of Egypt, you will worship God on this mountain."

At this point, Moses lacked confidence; his youthful zeal for his compatriots had long vanished. He immediately came up with a series of questions and excuses. First, he attempted to disqualify himself by saying, "Who am I? How can I bear this heavy responsibility?"

Remember this wasn't how Moses once responded when he witnessed the plight of his people (Exodus 2). He stood up boldly for his fellow Israelites even without God's command. However, his approach backfired, causing him to retreat and doubt his own inadequacies for the task. It's vital to remember that we should never decide whether to respond to God's calling based on our self-perceived talents and capacities. Our self-assessment is never reliable.

A calling is when God sees a need in people, decides to extend His grace, and takes action. We are merely His instruments and channels. Yet we often make ourselves the centre of the calling, focusing on what we want to do or what we're good at. The crucial factor isn't who we are, but who God is. God's response to Moses's self-doubt was clear: "I will be with you." What was critical was not Moses's capability. but God's presence. We need to shift our focus from ourselves to God and His faithfulness.

Confirmation of calling: God's presence

Ultimately, when God calls, He equips and prepares. He provides all that we need to fulfil His calling. Our part is to trust in Him, to rely on His presence and faithfulness, and to be willing to obediently respond to His call. In Exodus 3" 12–13, we read:

> ¹² And God said, "I will be with you. And this will be the sign to you that it is I who have sent you: when you have brought the people out of Egypt, you will worship God on this mountain."
>
> ¹³ Moses said to God, "Suppose I go to the Israelites and say to them, 'The God of your fathers has sent me to you,' and they ask me, 'What is his name?' Then what shall I tell them?"

In the Old Testament, God's presence was not an abstract idea but a tangible experience, signifying His power alongside humanity. So, when God assured Moses of His constant presence, He foretold that after Moses led the Israelites out, they would "worship me (God) on this mountain."

How did God answer Moses's question? He told Moses:

> I AM WHO I AM. This is what you are to say to the Israelites: "I AM has sent me to you." (v. 14)

This was like handing Moses an authorisation or court order, affirming that his qualification to lead the Israelites out of Egypt stemmed from being chosen by God Himself, whose name is "I am." The translation of God's name in the Chinese Bible captures part of its essence – "I am forever unchanging", highlighting His steadfastness. His words and His will remain constant, never varying or wavering.

We must not confine God. Remember Jacob? During his encounter with God, he asked to know God's name, yet God did not disclose it because He is not confined by anyone's understanding or expectations. This is an essential concept of creation. God created humanity in His image, and we cannot play God or manipulate Him. God is beyond human control and comprehension. But we know what God says will come to pass. This is His promise. We can absolutely trust Him.

Therefore, the key to understanding calling lies not in who we are, but in who God is – He is completely faithful, utterly reliable, intimately acquainted with us, and He is the very One who created us. This is the fundamental concept of calling. Following God's calling can be full of uncertainties or unanswered questions, but it doesn't matter because God's faithfulness is absolutely certain. That's all we need to know.

Letting go of past baggage

In the past, Moses had made serious mistakes and impulsively killed an Egyptian. Compelled to flee, he ended up spending years in the wilderness. Yet, this experience served a critical purpose. Having been a pampered prince within palace walls, Moses was used to a life of luxury. God, in his infinite wisdom, cast him into the wilderness for forty years to prepare him for his life-long calling. Four decades of shepherding in the wilderness effectively gifted Moses with invaluable survival skills as well as humility, shaping him into someone who was capable of guiding God's people out of slavery and writing God's Law. What initially appeared to be a resounding failure, a loss of direction in life and a very dull job turned out to be immensely relevant to his calling later. This, indeed, was all part of God's grand design. God had been working in Moses's life from the day he was born, wonderfully equipping him for his calling.

A story was told of a young girl in London, England, in the early 1900s. While other children were lively and cheerful, she was often downcast because she was born with black hair, an uncommon trait among English people. Seeing her classmates with their beautiful blonde hair, she deeply resented her appearance. To add to her distress, she stopped growing at 4 feet 10 inches, which was significantly shorter than everyone else. Looking at her reflection in the mirror, this small girl despised herself and even blamed God for creating her this way.

As she grew up, God called her to serve as a missionary in China. The voyage from England to China spanned several months over land and ocean. After a long and arduous trip, when her ship finally arrived at a seaport in China, she rushed to the ship deck to take a look at the shore. In front of her was a bustling pier filled with people, all had black hair, and all were barely 5 feet tall. At that moment, she couldn't help but exclaim, "Lord, you had always known what you were doing."

If you know anything about the socio-political conditions of China in the early 1900s, you would know how difficult it was for any westerner to settle in China at that time due to a wave of xenophobia that swept across the nation. But this English woman, with a physique and hair resembling the Chinese, was readily accepted. Prior to this, she had never understood why God created her the way she was. Now, it all became clear to her. This self-loathing girl became a celebrated missionary – Gladys Aylward – the real-life inspiration behind the movie *The Inn of the Sixth Happiness*.

In our lives, we often encounter unchangeable circumstances that may seem random and even purposeless when viewed from our limited perspective. Yet in creation, it is the Creator who determines what is truly good. Since we cannot foresee the future and our vision is inherently narrow, we are prone to complaining. It's essential to recognise that our setbacks in life may be unique conditions given to us by God, serving as the instruments He will use for His glory. His work in our lives doesn't always involve extraordinary means or events; rather, it is a continuous process that shapes us, much like how God had been quietly preparing Moses all along.

Only God knows what the calling takes

In Exodus 4:10, Moses told the Lord:

> "Pardon your servant, Lord. I have never been eloquent, neither in the past nor since you have spoken to your servant. I am slow of speech and tongue."

To be honest, who in the world could negotiate with Pharaoh and outwit him? Only God could. Moses grew up in the palace and knew Pharaoh's power firsthand. He was also aware of his own limitations and recognised that he was "slow of speech and tongue". In fact, the original Hebrew text of this verse is rather incoherent: "I was . . . I will be . . . In other words . . ." Truly, Moses had difficulty speaking articulately.

But how did God respond? In verses 11–12, we read:

> 11 The Lord said to him, "Who gave human beings their mouths? Who makes them deaf or mute? Who gives them sight or makes them blind? Is it not I, the Lord? 12 Now go; I will help you speak and will teach you what to say."

Ironically, what Moses worried about most initially – his eloquence in speech – turned out to be irrelevant throughout the entire narrative of Exodus. In Moses's multiple interactions and debates with Pharaoh, it was ultimately God's divine intervention that led to the Israelites' liberation. Everything hinged on God's power and mercy.

We often fall into the trap of relying on our limited understanding, passing judgment on what we deem useful or not in our lives. We like to label which skills or life experiences are valuable and which ones are wasted. Yet, only God knows what we truly need when we respond to His calling. Moses didn't need eloquent speech. Therefore, God didn't need to grant it to him. What Moses really needed was God's presence, obedience and, later during his 40 years in the wilderness, A LOT of patience. In the end, Moses's biggest challenge wasn't Pharaoh, but rather the Israelites. Who could put up with 2 million stiff-necked, moaning people in the wilderness for 40 years? No one, other than the Moses God had equipped and called. God knew all of this. His meticulous preparation and moulding of Moses over his first 80 years of life were all part of His perfect plan. God always knows what He's doing.

16

The Donkey Jesus Rode On

In this chapter, we will explore a fascinating account of how God employed an animal for a specific purpose. Found in both Luke's and Matthew's accounts of Jesus's triumphant entry into Jerusalem on a donkey (Luke 19:28–44; Matthew 21:1–9), it's intriguing to note that both authors allocate a substantial portion of their narratives to record how Jesus instructed his disciples to bring him a specific donkey. Surprisingly, this part of the story seems to receive even more attention than Jesus's actual entry into Jerusalem itself. Clearly, the process of obtaining the donkey held profound significance in the eyes of these biblical authors.

Let's read Luke's account:

> [28] After Jesus had said this, he went on ahead, going up to Jerusalem. [29] As he approached Bethphage and Bethany at the hill called the Mount of Olives, he sent two of his disciples, saying to them, [30] "Go to the village ahead of you, and as you enter it, you will find a colt tied there, which no-one has ever ridden. Untie it and bring it here. [31] If anyone asks you, 'Why are you untying it?' say, 'The Lord needs it.'"
>
> [32] Those who were sent ahead went and found it just as he had told them. [33] As they were untying the colt, its owners asked them,

"Why are you untying the colt?"

34 They replied, "The Lord needs it."

35 They brought it to Jesus, threw their cloaks on the colt and put Jesus on it. **36** As he went along, people spread their cloaks on the road. **37** When he came near the place where the road goes down the Mount of Olives, the whole crowd of disciples began joyfully to praise God in loud voices for all the miracles they had seen:

38 "Blessed is the king who comes in the name of the Lord!"

"Peace in heaven and glory in the highest!"

39 Some of the Pharisees in the crowd said to Jesus, "Teacher, rebuke your disciples!"

40 "I tell you," he replied, "if they keep quiet, the stones will cry out."

41 As he approached Jerusalem and saw the city, he wept over it **42** and said, "If you, even you, had only known on this day what would bring you peace – but now it is hidden from your eyes. **43** The days will come upon you when your enemies will build an embankment against you and encircle you and hem you in on every side. **44** They will dash you to the ground, you and the children within your walls. They will not leave one stone on another, because you did not recognise the time of God's coming to you."

Jesus commissioned his disciples to bring a young donkey to him, and the instructions appeared rather straightforward. He told them that they would encounter a tied donkey and they should untie it. If someone questioned their intentions, their response should merely be, "The Lord needs it." The disciples followed his command, and remarkably, events unfolded exactly as predicted. The animal's owner easily agreed to let go of his animal after they said, "The Lord needs it." Jesus had arranged and orchestrated all the details beforehand. Afterwards, a large crowd of people joined them in hailing Jesus as their king and praising God. It's an exhilarating scene of collective worship.

Many Christians I know desire their lives to unfold in the same way as this story does – having God foretell all the details of their lives and exactly what they need to do or say in each situation. They believe that as long as they know the specific instructions from God, their lives and ministries will go smoothly and yield the right results. Wouldn't this be wonderful? Life becomes predictable and there's no need to worry about what to do and how to serve God. However, this is not the primary message of the passage.

Consider this question: Where else in the Gospel of Luke can we find a story where God also provided people with precise instructions on what to look for? It's found in the famous Christmas story. In Luke chapter 2, shepherds watching their flock by night near Bethlehem suddenly found themselves surrounded by a great light, and an angel instructed them to look for a very specific sign: "a baby wrapped in cloths and lying in a manger" (Luke 2:12). Then a spectacular scene of an army of heavenly hosts worshipping and praising God together appeared. Faithfully following the instructions, the shepherds discovered everything to be exactly as the angels had foretold. These shepherds became key witnesses to the arrival of the Messiah.

If you read both accounts carefully, you will realise that the main point of these two accounts is neither in the details of the instructions nor in how the predictions unfold as predicted. The real focus is not really on the donkey or the manger, but on the subsequent act of the people acknowledging Jesus as King and praising God together. Both stories are orchestrated by God as a plan to bring glory to Himself. It's not about the 'how' but the 'why'.

It's not about the 'how' but the 'why'

In our walk with God, how often do we merely focus on the 'how' instead of the 'why'? Our minds are constantly worrying about details, steps, methods, strategies, and results. Why do you think God chose a donkey? Indeed, one obvious answer is that it was a gentle and lowly animal often associated with serving meekly. Another practical reason is that riding on a donkey instead of a horse avoided provoking suspicion and reactions from the

Roman authorities. Actually, however, Scripture tells us exactly what God wanted to communicate by a man coming on a donkey. It was a well-known prophecy that would readily come to the mind of the Jewish people of that time. Zechariah clearly foretold:

> See, your king comes to you, righteous and victorious, lowly and riding on a donkey, on a colt, the foal of a donkey. (9:9)

The prophecy states that the one coming on a donkey is not someone who's going to be king later, but the one who is *already* the victorious king. Jesus's riding on a donkey was not only to show his humility but, more importantly, his kingship. Up until this point, Jesus had maintained a discreet profile to avoid inciting misunderstanding or rebellions. However, during the final week of His life, Jesus chose to stage this poignant scene, asserting His identity as the prophesied King in Scripture. His entrance into Jerusalem signified the fulfilment of ancient prophecies and God's covenant with Abraham and David.

The foundation of our calling lies in the fact that our Lord is already the victorious King. When we think of our calling or ministries, we often focus too much on ourselves. We question if we are capable, if our efforts will bear fruit, or if the intended results can be achieved. We serve Jesus as if his kingship depends on how we do things. In Luke chapters 2 and 19, neither the shepherds nor the disciples had anything to worry about. They only needed to be ready to follow God's prompts, witness God's glory and join in the act of praising God together. We are never called to struggle our way through serving him or to worry about whether our work will yield the results God wants. Regardless of what we do, the one thing we should truly focus on is recognising He has already won the battle, and how He has prepared everything for His glory. Both the initiatives and the results depend solely on God, not on us. He is both the Alpha and the Omega. This shift in perspectives changes everything.

However, God also loves to involve us in His work. This is the beauty of creation and the essence of calling – He's calling us to partner with Him in

His work and plans. This is why Jesus commissioned his disciples to find the donkey and bring it to him even though he was fully capable of doing it himself.

Observe carefully the contrast between the verbs used to describe Jesus's role in the story: 'send' and 'say'; and the verbs depicting the disciples' role: 'go', 'enter', 'find', 'reply', 'bring it to Jesus' and 'put Jesus on it'. On the surface, it may seem as though the disciples were the ones actively shaping the event. Despite Jesus's seemingly passive role in the beginning of the story, notice how the passage emphasises that it was not the disciples who had prepared the donkey for Jesus; rather it was Jesus who had already prepared it for them. Jesus was the one in full control. Our King has made all the preparations for us. Are we ready to work with Him? Serving the Lord is not a burdensome task; we simply need to remember that our Lord is already the King. Looking back at my past ministries, I realise that God had already arranged everything behind the scenes – He is the Boss we can fully trust.

What do we know about the donkey?

Intriguingly, Luke's narrative provides extensive detail about this particular donkey. First, we know that the donkey was tied. It lived a restricted life at the mercy of others. Second, no one had ever ridden on this donkey before (v. 30). There are two possible conclusions we can reach from this statement. One is that this donkey was too young, and two, it was somewhat weak and inexperienced. When the owner asked the disciples why they were untying it, the question probably meant, "Why would you choose this one instead of the other better ones available?"

Matthew's account of this story gives us more details of the situation: another animal (most likely its mother) had to accompany the donkey while it was being ridden by Jesus (Matthew 21:5–7). So this donkey was too young or too inexperienced for the task. It simply didn't qualify to be independently ridden. A grown man riding on a weak donkey isn't an impressive scene. Surely in first-century Palestine, Jesus should have had plenty of better donkeys at his disposal. But he specifically chose this one. Jesus didn't choose to ride on a horse. In fact, he didn't even choose a capable donkey.

Another possible explanation for why no one had ever ridden this donkey before is that it was customary for kings in ancient civilisations to never use anything that had been used by someone else. This point is also highlighted later when Luke states that the tomb belonging to Joseph of Arimathea had never been used by anyone before Jesus's body was laid inside (Luke 23:53). From this angle, Jesus's choice of a donkey that has never been ridden also confirms his royal kingship.

Despite our weaknesses and inadequacies, God has chosen us. And therein lies the marvel: we are chosen to bring glory to Him, but through humility and obedience. The donkey certainly looked ridiculous to the Pharisees. But the donkey's mission was not to make the Pharisees happy or to fit in to the people's false expectations of the Messiah. Its mission was simply to let people recognise Jesus as the one Scripture had been pointing to.

Regardless of whether we receive praise or criticism, agreement or opposition, our aim should not be to cater to human expectations, preferences or public opinion. Rather, our aim should be to align ourselves with God, so that the King's triumphant fulfilment of the Old Testament prophecies may be revealed, enabling others to recognise Him as their King and willingly accept Him as their Lord. This is the most significant call of our lives.

Imagine you are the donkey. How would you feel when you are brought to Jesus and have Jesus riding on you? Our natural instinct would be, as always, to worry about whether we're qualified to accomplish the mission or how to do it. Of course the donkey was not qualified. No one is ever worthy to serve Jesus. There's no question about that. You are called to serve him only because Jesus has chosen to use you for his glory.

As you slowly enter Jerusalem, you witness all the cheers and praises the crowd shouts. The crowd welcomes him with joy, laying their garments on the path as a symbol of his majesty and royalty. As the donkey, you may feel a sense of honour, but it is crucial to recognise that the adoration and cheers are not directed toward you but toward the Lord you are carrying on your back. When we serve God and people, there may be times when we receive admiration and praise from others. However, let us not allow these accolades to cloud our judgment or inflate our egos. The ultimate purpose of our service is not to bring glory to ourselves, but to our King, the only one who deserves our worship and devotion.

Beyond the cheers

While the Christmas story in Luke 2 and the story of Jesus entering Jerusalem as King share some significant similarities, there is one subtle difference. In 19:38, the people shouted:

> "Blessed is the king who comes in the name of the Lord!
>   Peace in heaven and glory in the highest!"

These words bear a resemblance to the proclamation of the angels in Bethlehem at Jesus's birth. However, in 2:14, it is explicitly stated:

> "Glory to God in the highest heaven,
>   and on earth peace to those on whom his favour rests."

There should be glory in heaven and peace on earth. Yet, this peace on earth is not mentioned in chapter 19, possibly indicating that peace was not yet established at that time. Luke's Gospel depicts Jesus Christ as the victorious King who has overcome death and sin, enabling reconciliation between humanity and God. True peace and glory exist in heaven, and those who believe in the Lord can experience peace on earth as well. However, the absence of peace on earth is significant as Jesus was about to enter Jerusalem, where he would soon face rejection from his own people and death on the cross.

However, we're immediately reminded that praising God is our ultimate goal. In verse 40, Jesus declared that if his disciples remain silent, the stones would cry out in praise. In other words, it was impossible for the disciples to remain silent and not praise the Lord. This is the same for us. The purpose of the church's existence is to exalt this King, for he is already the victorious King. He desires to enter our hearts, our churches and our communities.

Verses 41–44 mention Jesus's arrival in Jerusalem. Upon seeing the city, he wept. This passage provides a striking contrast to the preceding verses, 35–38, where there was much celebration. The crowd witnessed the exultant entry of the King into Jerusalem, a scene of glory and worship. However, they were unable to foresee the great calamity that would befall Jerusalem, which was the reason Jesus wept for the city. While the people rejoiced, Jesus wept, reminding us not to let other people's cheers and noises blind us to the reality that God sees.

Jesus is our King, and he eagerly desires to reign in our lives. We are like humble donkeys, meant to usher in the praise for the King. He seeks to work through you as His vessel, shining His glory on earth. This is the heart of the Great Commission: The King is calling and commissioning us to go out and make him known. Are we ready to respond to this call?

IX

Is the Lord calling you? (Part 2)

An ordinary voice from an extraordinary God

17

Samuel

Over the many years of my ministry, I have met numerous Christians who have told me how much they long to hear God's voice. Their desire stems from a genuine, heartfelt longing to experience God and understand His will clearly. They wonder why they can't 'hear' His voice (despite having the whole Bible on their shelves) and find themselves seeking new ways to increase their chances of hearing something from above. If we look at all the stories in the Bible where someone heard God's voice clearly, we'll notice that in the vast majority of these stories, the people who heard God's message weren't seeking a message from God at the time. Some of them weren't even anticipating hearing anything from God at all. Most of them were just doing what they normally did every day.

Many Christians wish they could hear God calling their names and giving them guidance on what to do next, just like Samuel heard God calling his name repeatedly "Samuel, Samuel . . ." In this chapter, let's look at the story in 1 Samuel 3:1–18 in greater detail and see how it teaches us important lessons about hearing God's call.

[1] The boy Samuel ministered before the Lord under Eli. In those days the word of the Lord was rare; there were not many visions.

² One night Eli, whose eyes were becoming so weak that he could barely see, was lying down in his usual place. ³ The lamp of God had not yet gone out, and Samuel was lying down in the house of the Lord, where the ark of God was. ⁴ Then the Lord called Samuel. Samuel answered, "Here I am."

⁵ And he ran to Eli and said, "Here I am; you called me."

But Eli said, "I did not call; go back and lie down." So he went and lay down.

⁶ Again the Lord called, "Samuel!" And Samuel got up and went to Eli and said, "Here I am; you called me."

"My son," Eli said, "I did not call; go back and lie down."

⁷ Now Samuel did not yet know the Lord: The word of the Lord had not yet been revealed to him.

⁸ A third time the Lord called, "Samuel!" And Samuel got up and went to Eli and said, "Here I am; you called me."

Then Eli realised that the Lord was calling the boy. ⁹ So Eli told Samuel, "Go and lie down, and if he calls you, say, 'Speak, Lord, for your servant is listening.'" So Samuel went and lay down in his place.

¹⁰ The Lord came and stood there, calling as at the other times, "Samuel! Samuel!"

Then Samuel said, "Speak, for your servant is listening."

¹¹ And the Lord said to Samuel: "See, I am about to do something in Israel that will make the ears of everyone who hears about it tingle. ¹² At that time I will carry out against Eli everything I spoke against his family – from beginning to end. ¹³ For I told him that I would judge his family forever because of the sin he knew about; his sons blasphemed God, and he failed to restrain them. ¹⁴ Therefore I swore to the house of Eli, 'The guilt of Eli's house will never be atoned for by sacrifice or offering.'"

When the Word of the Lord is scarce

The passage paints the backdrop for the story: "In those days the word of the Lord was rare; there were not many visions" (3:1). God's voice seemed scarce, much like in our present generation, when people are spiritually deaf and unwilling to listen to God's words. Even believers are increasingly tuned to alternative voices from the world, becoming indifferent to God's Word.

Why couldn't Samuel's generation hear from God? The answer lies in what God revealed to Samuel (vv. 11–13). God had spoken to the priest Eli, but he turned a deaf ear. Priests were the mouthpieces of God. On Sabbaths and festivals, the priests would gather the people before the tent to teach God's law. People could have heard God's Word through this proper channel, just like we hear God's Word today through the church, fellowship and worship. The issue was that even those who were meant to be paying the closest attention to God's Word did not obey it.

When the will to listen is lacking, the opportunity to hear is certainly scarce. God told Samuel that what He had spoken to Eli would now be fulfilled. God's conversation with Samuel can be understood in the context of the preceding book, Judges. During the era of the judges, God also seemed to be silent. People did as they pleased; no one listened to God. In Samuel's time, a new era began in which God formally established the role of the prophets. This passage records the first time God called a prophet to be His mouthpiece. This was God's calling for Samuel's life.

God's call to Samuel took four attempts to connect. In verse 11, the Lord said to Samuel, "See, I am about to do something in Israel that will make the ears of everyone who hears about it tingle." This statement is critical. In the original Hebrew text, the 'something' that God intends to do is actually the same word as the 'Word' mentioned in verse 1. God's Word, when ignored, transforms into action – a judgment upon Eli. 'Tingle' here means to be extremely astonished. God's Word, once spoken, wouldn't just be a warning anymore; it would manifest in action. It implies deep shock.

Today, when we do not heed God's commands, the consequences gradually become visible in our community and society. People only start to listen when they experience these consequences directly, and Christians are no exception to this. It often takes frequent tragedies in families and in our communities to shock us into the realisation that we haven't been obeying God's Word, the church hasn't been following God's commands, and we've failed to be light and salt for the world.

What God says will inevitably come to pass. This story teaches us that God's words must not be taken lightly. But God is also a merciful God and will not give up on His people. Even when people turn a deaf ear, He continues to call until they hear Him, just as He did with Samuel and Eli. Have we heard God's call? Perhaps God has been speaking to you for a long time, but you haven't taken it in. God won't give up.

To put it another way, the problem of this generation is not that God no longer speaks. The problem is that we are accustomed to not listening. We must learn from this passage how to listen to God's call. Only by allowing God's message to enter our hearts can we find the strength to know and live out His call. How do we do it? We can learn four key lessons from Samuel.

Being ready anytime, anywhere

The passage elaborates on how Samuel heard God's voice. The voice calling Samuel's name was repeated three times before Samuel understood its source. But each time, Samuel's response was the same: "Here I am."

Even though Samuel originally thought it was Eli, not God, calling him, he still responded with "Here I am" each time (vv. 4, 6, 8). This "Here I am" doesn't just mean reporting in. It is saying, "I am ready, please give your command." Being prepared to listen at all times is the first attitude we need to have. If we assume God no longer speaks to us today, we won't have a heart ready to listen at any time.

The passage gives us some interesting details before the story begins, which might seem irrelevant, but they are important. In verses 2 to 3:

> ² One night Eli, whose eyes were becoming so weak that he could barely see, was lying down in his usual place. ³ The lamp of God had not yet gone out, and Samuel was lying down in the house of the Lord, where the ark of God was.

Eli was "lying down in his usual place" and couldn't see properly. What about Samuel? The author specifically points out that he was lying down where the Ark of God was, where the lamp never went out. What was the significance of this?

By drawing our attention to the lamp of God that hadn't gone out, the author is intentionally highlighting a contrast between where Eli and Samuel were sleeping. This piece of background information is crucial. The Ark was placed in the Most Holy Place of the Tabernacle, and the lamp inside the Tabernacle had to burn continuously, twenty-four hours a day (Exodus 27:20–21; Leviticus 24:2). There were no electric lights back then; people used oil lamps. How did they ensure an oil lamp burned continuously without going out? Someone had to be present and awake to tend to it, adding oil when needed. Samuel's responsibility was to make sure the lamp never went out in the place where the Ark was kept. This was the priest's duty, but Eli's failing eyesight prevented him from doing it, so he had entrusted this task to Samuel.

The passage makes clear that Samuel was attending in the house of the Lord where the Ark was, where the lamp was always burning. Eli had ceased fulfilling his responsibilities, and Samuel had assumed his role. Moreover, Samuel wasn't truly sleeping; the term 'lying down' actually means 'lying still', so he was one who was vigilant and watching the lamp of God. This holds symbolic meaning. Eli not only had weak physical eyesight, his spiritual sight was also dimmed; he had become blind to the spiritual state of his family and his people.

Samuel's readiness to respond at any moment serves as a valuable lesson for us. The passage emphasises that Samuel was able to hear God's voice because he was ready at all times, prepared to answer and obey immediately.

Are you prepared? Do you know that God can call you at any time? If you're not prepared, you won't be able to hear Him clearly. "Waiting" isn't about being idle, only to snap to attention when God's command comes. Rather, it is an attitude – a yearning to listen and be prepared to act upon what you hear. Anyone who has interacted with children understands this principle. When a parent asks their child to do something, if the child isn't in the mood, they might pretend not to hear. Yet, if the same parent whispers "ice cream" softly, the child hears and reacts instantly. We tend to hear what we desire to hear. When our minds get cluttered with countless desires and worries, we become unprepared to receive God's message.

I don't know what God's call is for you, whether it's like Eli's, calling you to repent, or like Samuel's, asking you to take on certain responsibilities. Whatever it is, the important thing is that you are always ready to listen. Every time you attend worship, listen to a sermon or open the Bible, do you ask yourself: "What does God want to say to me today?" It's a simple thing, yet we rarely do it.

Putting aside our own presumptions about calling

Our hearts often gravitate towards hearing what aligns with our desires, making them resistant to truly listening. They are clouded by numerous misconceptions and personal presumptions about what God may or may not call us to do. However, since God's ways and thoughts are higher than ours, we must let go of our preconceptions.

In Samuel's time, only Levites were eligible to become priests. Since Samuel wasn't a Levite, how was he able to follow Eli to become a priest? This was because his mother Hannah dedicated him to the Lord from birth. In ancient Israel, firstborn sons could be consecrated to the Lord as priests and trained to serve God in the temple. This was exactly Samuel's situation. If you were Samuel, knowing Eli was in his old age, and you heard God calling you, you would naturally assume God must be calling you to become a priest. Every facet of his life seemed to point in this direction. However, God had a different plan. God called him to be a prophet instead.

If you hear God calling your name repeatedly, you might expect God to have a very exciting message for you or a grand mission for your life. In Samuel's case, however, God was calling Samuel to pronounce a solemn judgment on Eli and his family. This was indeed a difficult and unexpected mission for a young boy who was still under Eli's guidance and care. Eli was a father figure to him.

Very often, we set our own agendas for our lives, expecting God's calling for us to come in a certain way at a certain time. But God's intentions are often entirely different from our thoughts. His ways are higher than our ways. Today, what God calls us to do might be something we have never considered.

For instance, when the church extends an invitation for fellow believers to serve, it's common for many to adopt a humble appearance, saying, "Other people are better than me, why would it be me? I can't do it; I have so many problems . . ." We convince ourselves that God wouldn't choose us to do things we don't want to do, and consequently, we inadvertently tune out God's voice. We also tend to find excuses, allowing distractions to divert our hearts elsewhere. It's crucial that we remove our preconceived notions and simply say to God, "Here I am," ready to listen to His call with an open mind and heart.

Learning to discern is a step-by-step journey

Later, when Eli realised that the voice could be the Lord calling the boy, he instructed Samuel on how to respond to God's voice:

> So Eli told Samuel, "Go and lie down, and if he calls you, say, 'Speak, Lord, for your servant is listening.'" (v. 9)

Why couldn't Samuel recognise it was God calling him if he had a humble, open heart? Wasn't he willing to listen? Verse 7 tells us that Samuel didn't recognise the voice of the Lord because he "did not yet know the Lord". Having followed Eli and taken on the role of a priest, how could Samuel not know the Lord? Here, 'knowing' doesn't mean unfamiliarity. The subsequent phrase "the word of the Lord had not yet been revealed to him" clarifies that Samuel hadn't personally heard God speak to him directly yet. Eli had, but Samuel hadn't. Thus, he wasn't aware that God could communicate with him in this way. Even Samuel, a great prophet of the Lord, once had to take baby steps in learning how to hear from the Lord.

When God called Samuel, it probably sounded just like Eli's voice, leading Samuel to assume that Eli was the one calling him. God's call doesn't usually come in a spectacular or extraordinary manner. We often think that God hasn't called us because we expect His call to be dramatic or supernatural. However, in reality, God likes to call us through ordinary, everyday experiences. There might be exceptional moments when God uses more extraordinary ways to call His people, but most of the time He doesn't. God called Samuel in an ordinary way, so ordinary that he confused it with the same voice he heard every day. This reminds us to stay attuned to God, recognising that His voice might be found in the most commonplace events of life.

God can communicate with you through a variety of channels, such as the Bible, a sermon or a specific verse or statement that resonates deeply with you. I've experienced this during preaching. Sometimes, a single ordinary line I've said – perhaps even one I hadn't planned on saying – may profoundly affect a listener.

God's voice might also come through casual comments, even those from non-believers, or through recent happenings, challenges or stories of others. These seemingly insignificant moments may carry God's message. Always be prepared to hear Him with a sensitive heart, and you will grow in wisdom in discerning His voice.

Acting upon it

We need to listen and, more importantly, obey:

> **15** Samuel lay down until morning and then opened the doors of the house of the Lord. He was afraid to tell Eli the vision, **16** but Eli called him and said, "Samuel, my son."
>
> Samuel answered, "Here I am."
>
> **17** "What was it he said to you?" Eli asked. "Do not hide it from me. May God deal with you, be it ever so severely, if you hide from me anything he told you." **18** So Samuel told him everything, hiding nothing from him. Then Eli said, "He is the Lord; let him do what is good in his eyes." (1 Samuel 3:15–18)

Eli previously heard God's messages but didn't obey. In both the Old and New Testaments, the words 'listen' and 'obey' are essentially the same word. To listen means to follow. To be considered obedient, a Christian must not only lend an ear to instructions but also take action upon them. Otherwise, how do you distinguish yourself from someone who hears nothing at all?

Furthermore, the Greek word 'Word' also holds a double meaning – it also means 'the way'. God's Word is a way to be walked in and lived out, not just spoken. Mere speech is insufficient; merely hearing is also inadequate. Simply understanding intellectually without practical action means you haven't truly understood. We may have read God's Word and understood much of it, but until we practically live it out in our lives, it isn't truly ours.

Unlike Eli, who heard but didn't heed, Samuel listened attentively and obeyed. First, when Eli instructed him to respond to God, Samuel followed precisely. Then when God entrusted him with a message for Eli, he neither hid the truth from Eli nor attempted to tone down the severity of God's message, though it was a deeply challenging message to deliver. He faithfully relayed exactly what he had received from God. This is what a prophet is called to do – to communicate God's words accurately as they are received no matter how difficult the message is.

Through readiness and obedience, Samuel took on the first mission of his prophetic journey and became a prophet for God at a time when God's people desperately needed to hear from God once again.

18

David

Another noteworthy biblical character who offers valuable insights into God's calling is David. David's life stands in stark contrast to that of Moses. While Moses led the nation across the Red Sea and the wilderness with wonders and signs, David's life lacked spectacular supernatural experiences. According to the book of Samuel, David never performed any miracles. His most remarkable feat was defeating Goliath, but the rest of his life was marked by a multitude of struggles. For decades, he was pursued either by Saul, his own son or other enemies. His relationships with his children were in shambles, especially with his son Absalom, who never had a chance to redeem himself. David's life eventually ended in a state of melancholy. God never miraculously intervened to remove his misery.

Furthermore, David's life was marked by weaknesses and corruption. He once indulged in lust and became entangled in violence, adultery and even murder – a storyline worthy of an R-rated film. After his daughter was assaulted by his son, he failed to pursue justice for her and allowed the matter to remain unresolved. He also appeared powerless in the face of his own son's betrayal. You may say that God had picked the right person to write the Psalms. But if we assume that God chose David because of his exemplary character, we would be mistaken. He was as messy as the rest of us.

Yet God still chose him and called him to be a significant part of His plan for the world. God's grace is sufficient even for David. This is the essence of God's calling.

God works with messiness

Let us examine 1 Samuel 16 – the story of Samuel anointing David as king. In verses 1–5:

> [1] The Lord said to Samuel, "How long will you mourn for Saul, since I have rejected him as king over Israel? Fill your horn with oil and be on your way; I am sending you to Jesse of Bethlehem. I have chosen one of his sons to be king."
>
> [2] But Samuel said, "How can I go? If Saul hears about it, he will kill me." The Lord said, "Take a heifer with you and say, 'I have come to sacrifice to the Lord.' [3] Invite Jesse to the sacrifice, and I will show you what to do. You are to anoint for me the one I indicate." [4] Samuel did what the Lord said. When he arrived at Bethlehem, the elders of the town trembled when they met him. They asked, "Do you come in peace?"
>
> [5] Samuel replied, "Yes, in peace; I have come to sacrifice to the Lord. Consecrate yourselves and come to the sacrifice with me." Then he consecrated Jesse and his sons and invited them to the sacrifice.

Initially, God chose Saul as the king, but Saul failed to remain faithful to God. When the Lord commanded Samuel to anoint a new leader, Samuel was disheartened and questioned the decision: "How can I go?" Samuel was fully aware that Saul, characterised by his ambition and envy of others' abilities, would not relinquish his throne without a fight. Despite his esteemed position as a prophet, Samuel harboured fear towards Saul and hesitated to immediately obey God. In the end, God had to give him more specific instructions on how to proceed to avoid Saul's retaliation.

Thus, the circumstances surrounding David's anointing were rather unfortunate. Having been chosen by God and anointed by Samuel, David should have been immediately elevated to the position of king. However, it came at an inconvenient time when Saul was hostile to anyone who posed a threat to his reign. David led a life filled with challenges and unwanted enemies.

But David didn't need to wait until his messy life was sorted out before receiving God's calling. It is precisely because of David's struggles and failures that he knew how to hold tightly onto God's faithfulness. God's power and glory were revealed through David's disordered life.

We often hear Christians say, "Everything in my life would have been so different if it weren't for . . ." Or they may say, "My life is quite jumbled up now. I'll wait until all these obstacles are cleared before I respond to God's calling." It's important to recognise that every aspect of our existence is under God's control. It's God who is at work, not us. Calling is all about God's grace and power working through our shortcomings. What matters is how we view these obstacles from God's perspective, ensuring that they do not paralyse us or prevent us from moving forward.

The truth is, God has already chosen the people He wants to use, regardless of their shortcomings. His calling has room for obstacles because His grace is always sufficient.

God always sees beyond what we see

Samuel proceeded to choose a successor to the throne among Jesse's sons:

> **6** When they arrived, Samuel saw Eliab and thought, "Surely the Lord's anointed stands here before the Lord." **7** But the Lord said to Samuel, "Do not consider his appearance or his height, for I have rejected him. The Lord does not look at the things people look at. People look at the outward appearance, but the Lord looks at the heart."

In verses 6–7, Samuel still carried the burden of Saul in his heart. Saul stood tall and impressive, and Eliab possessed a strong physique. It was only natural for Samuel to think, "Isn't this the one whom the Lord has chosen?" Preconceived notions often hinder us from discerning God's will.

The end of verse 7 says, "People look at the outward appearance, but the Lord looks at the heart." It is a common belief that God selected David because he was "a man after [His] own heart" (Acts 13:22). However, aside from his readiness to trust and obey God, David's actions in real life often contradicted God's will. The Bible does not portray David as particularly obedient, outstanding or exceptional. Instead, it underscores the idea that what God sees is what truly matters. God's choice rested on someone who resonated with His heart, or simply put, someone chosen "according to My will". It's as if God is stating, "I will choose whomever I deem fit, according to My will."

What about Jesse's other sons? Let's look at verses 8–11:

> **8** Then Jesse called Abinadab and made him pass in front of Samuel. But Samuel said, "The Lord has not chosen this one either." **9** Jesse then made Shammah pass by, but Samuel said, "Nor has the Lord chosen this one."
>
> **10** Jesse made seven of his sons pass before Samuel, but Samuel said to him, "The Lord has not chosen these." **11** So he asked Jesse, "Are these all the sons you have?"
>
> "There is still the youngest," Jesse answered. "He is tending the sheep."
>
> Samuel said, "Send for him; we will not sit down until he arrives."

Some Bible translations may not fully capture the tone of Jesse's response in verse 11. In the original Hebrew text, when Samuel inquires if all his sons have arrived, Jesse's response includes the word 'behold'. Jesse's intention was not to say, "Look, he is busy working", but rather, "You go and take a look at him yourself; he's just a young shepherd boy, not worthy of your attention."

During that time, shepherding was considered the lowliest job, only given to the lowest-ranking individuals. David, being the youngest in the family, would never have been considered a viable candidate for anything important in the community, let alone the position of a king. Therefore, David not only suffered under Saul's rule, he was even despised by his own father who failed to account for him. Nevertheless, Samuel insisted on seeing the youngest son, and so David finally arrived.

In verse 12, we read:

> So he sent for him and had him brought in. He was glowing with health and had a fine appearance and handsome features. Then the Lord said, "Rise and anoint him; this is the one."

Notice how the author describes Jesse's sons. Starting with the eldest, the first three are named, while the next four are unnamed, indicating their insignificance. Only at the end of the passage is the youngest, David, indirectly mentioned (in the latter part of verse 13). This shows that David, in the eyes of the others, was insignificant.

Why does the passage specifically mention that David was "glowing with health and had a fine appearance and handsome features"? Does it mean that God prefers someone handsome over someone who's not? Not at all. The word 'handsome' used in the passage doesn't refer to physical attractiveness. It simply means 'a young lad' with youthful features. Later, when Goliath saw David's appearance (1 Samuel 17:42), he reacted with the same surprise. No wonder Goliath immediately scorned him, as he wasn't expecting the Israelites to send such a young boy to fight him. So, at that time, no one would have considered David a candidate for king. There was no reason to choose him. But that was what God did.

Let us continue with David's story. Saul, abandoned by God and tormented by evil spirits, summoned David to his presence. In 1 Samuel 16:14–18, it is recorded:

¹⁴ Now the Spirit of the Lord had departed from Saul, and an evil spirit from the Lord tormented him. ¹⁵ Saul's attendants told him, "See, an evil spirit from God is tormenting you. ¹⁶ Let our lord command his servants here to search for someone who can play the lyre. He will play when the evil spirit from God comes on you, and you will feel better."

¹⁷ So Saul said to his attendants, "Find someone who plays well and bring him to me."

¹⁸ One of the servants answered, "I have seen a son of Jesse of Bethlehem who knows how to play the lyre. He is a brave man and a warrior. He speaks well and is a fine-looking man. And the Lord is with him."

The passage does not provide further details, but it's evident that David's talents were closely tied to how God had shaped him in the wilderness over time. Playing the lyre, for example, was not a skill he possessed from birth; it required extensive practice. Tending to the flock could have been a monotonous task, yet David didn't waste this opportunity. He developed his skills in playing the lyre, writing psalms, and shooting stones with slings, probably unaware of the significance of these abilities at the time.

Furthermore, the official's introduction of David highlights other characteristics. The passage describes David as a "brave man". His courage had also been cultivated through years of training in the fields. As a shepherd, David had to single-handedly deal with wild beasts. He had to protect his flock with the simplest tools available. The phrase "he speaks well" implies that David, being the youngest among his older brothers, had learned to respond appropriately in many situations. Over time, he developed eloquence and graciousness in his interactions. "The Lord is with him" indicates an intimate relationship with God which others could observe.

Do we view our weaknesses through God's lens?

We are accustomed to viewing our weaknesses and work negatively, inventing numerous excuses why we are unfit to respond to God's calling. We're hooked by the idea that we should serve God in areas where we have gifts. However, this was not the case in the real-life stories of many biblical characters. God's calling itself is the gift. God has His own plans to use people's weaknesses for His glory. His greatness, not ours, is the focus. As Paul learned, it was through his weaknesses that he witnessed God's abundant grace (2 Corinthians 12:9).

Our God is a creative God, and we should not limit His actions by how we view our lives. David's life was marred by numerous failures. He was far from being a perfect candidate for God's sacred calling, but he learned from his pain, repented, and turned to God.

This isn't to imply that God likes our flaws and failures, but rather that God often delights in using our weaknesses to accomplish His work and reveal His glory. So, we can be totally honest and courageous when we reflect on our past experiences, even painful ones. Instead of rationalising or assigning blame on ourselves or others, we can seek God's grace within those experiences and understand their purpose, because His grace far surpasses our shortcomings. We'll never know how He will utilise us in the future unless we submit to Him fully in obedience.

Years ago in Hong Kong, a woman discovered she was pregnant. Facing extreme poverty, she contemplated aborting the child and even consumed multiple abortion pills, yet the baby inside her continued to grow. Doctors advised her to stop the pills and allow the child to be born. However, due to the excessive medication, the newborn girl required a blood transfusion immediately after birth and endured hardships from a young age. If you were that girl, how would you feel? Imagine growing up knowing that even your own mother didn't want you.

Thankfully, when the girl grew up, she found faith in Christ and God healed and restored her completely, enabling her to see her own life from a fresh perspective. She came to the profound realization that, despite the circumstances of her birth, God's unwavering determination brought her into existence. In her own words, she testified, "My mother may have tried everything to be rid of me, but God was resolute in His desire to have me!" Through this experience, she understood that her life was incredibly valuable in God's eyes, and her life was never the same again.

A mundane job used by God

David spent his early life as a shepherd, one of the most despised jobs in ancient times. This was why Jesse sent the youngest son in the family to do this job. A shepherd typically sat around the field watching over the sheep. When the sheep were safe, the shepherd would pick up an instrument and sing some tunes. When a predator came, he would pick up a slingshot to shoot. When the family needed to run some errands, he would get up to help. Such was David's everyday life as a shepherd boy, and this was the life God had chosen to use for His purposes. This ordinary and despised work environment turned out to be very significant in God's calling for David.

When Goliath challenged the Israelites in 1 Samuel 17, striking fear into the hearts of many, David showed no fear. His victory over the giant might be seen as a miracle, but if you read the text carefully, you'll realise on the day David defeated Goliath, everything he did was exactly what he had always done in a typical work week. He was simply attending to his elder brothers as usual when he heard Goliath's challenge. Then in the slaying of Goliath, both the skill and the weapon David used were the same skill and tool he often used in his day-to-day job. God had prepared David from day one. In 1 Samuel 17:40, we read:

> Then he took his staff in his hand, chose five smooth stones from the stream, put them in the pouch of his shepherd's bag and, with his sling in his hand, approached the Philistine.

The passage mentions that David "chose five smooth stones from the stream". Slingshot proficiency requires a lot of skill and practice. Choosing the right stones is an important part of the process as they need to be smooth and well-balanced to ensure accuracy and speed in slinging. I have personally visited the valley mentioned in the passage and tried selecting stones from the site. I struggled to find smooth, well-balanced stones! It is indeed a challenging task that requires experience and practice. If David hadn't taken his shepherding role seriously, not only would he have failed to defeat the giant, but he might also have jeopardised even his own life.

God's way of preparing and equipping David for his calling was not through dramatic miracles but rather through the most ordinary, 'insignificant' tasks he performed daily. Even the most mundane and tedious work can hold great value when used by God.

An ordinary life through the eyes of an extraordinary God

Have you ever wondered why David was able to write so many powerful, soul-stirring psalms? The hardships, pain and complexities he faced throughout his life had enabled him to humbly acknowledge his helplessness and his total dependence on God's mercy and faithfulness. His years of tending sheep in the lonely wilderness compelled him to pour out his heart to God and develop an intimate relationship with Him through prayers. Indeed, one of the most renowned prayers in history is Psalm 23, a timeless prayer of worship that has blessed millions of people for centuries. David's psalms have been a source of help and solace for many because they sprang from his personal struggles and the depths of his heart. It is through this genuine connection that his words can provide true comfort for us.

If we view our life experiences and work through our own lens, many things may seem meaningless and pointless. But we can adopt a different viewpoint and try to see them through the lens of God's grace. At first glance, David's triumph over Goliath and his ability to write great psalms may seem straightforward and effortless. However, all these are the product of years of God's meticulous work in painstakingly shaping a character through his experiences as a shepherd boy. David performed these seemingly ordinary and insignificant tasks with faithfulness and dedication. Remarkably, God used the ordinary tasks that David performed to fulfil His grand purpose.

Your lifelong calling from God may be related to your strengths and abilities, but it may also have a profound connection to your weaknesses, trials and seemingly insignificant experiences. God can use all of them for His glory.

X

Who sets your limit?

Rejecting boundaries not imposed by God

19

Jabez

The story of Jabez in the Bible had remained relatively obscure until Bruce Wilkinson's popular book, *The Prayer of Jabez*, cast a spotlight on it. Prior to this, Jabez and his prayer often went overlooked, buried within the early chapters of the book of Chronicles. These dense chapters of genealogical records don't typically captivate readers, causing many Christians to skim past them.

Generally, ancient genealogies follow a straightforward format, outlining familial relationships and lineages. However, nestled within these lists in 1 Chronicles 4, an unusual statement stands out and breaks the pattern in verse 9:

> Jabez was more honourable than his brothers. His mother had named him Jabez, saying, "I gave birth to him in pain."

Then, even more unusual, a prayer is included in the genealogy (v. 10):

> [10] Jabez cried out to the God of Israel, "Oh, that you would bless me and enlarge my territory! Let your hand be with me, and keep me from harm so that I will be free from pain." And God granted his request.

This segment about a man named Jabez and his prayers inserted into a lengthy genealogical account was a deliberate divergence from the norm and was exceptionally rare among ancient genealogical records. Whenever we encounter a peculiar literary arrangement that seems deliberate, we can expect that it wants to convey a significant message.

This isn't the only irregularity in this record. The first chapter of 1 Chronicles presents the genealogy of non-Israelite peoples. It's not until the second chapter that we find the genealogies of Israel's sons. However, the arrangement of the tribes is rather odd. Instead of starting with Reuben, Jacob's firstborn, it begins with Judah. What's the reason behind this?

When the name that defines you is 'pain'

A clue emerges in 1 Chronicles 5:2, where we learn that this genealogy was rewritten after the captivity. By that time, God had revealed that the promised Messiah would emerge from the lineage of David, who was from the tribe of Judah. Recognising the profound significance of this revelation, the author elevates the tribe of Judah in the records.

In this context, Jabez would be the most honourable person within the most distinguished tribe. What's the big deal about Jabez? Apart from these two verses, he is virtually absent from the Bible. We know almost nothing about him except for his prayer and that his birth had brought great pain to his mother.

This individual who was the most esteemed in all of Israel carried a rather uncomfortable name: he was named Jabez because his mother had borne him in pain (v. 9). In the original Hebrew text, 'Jabez' literally means 'pain,' with only a single letter variation. Certainly, it was Jabez's mother who endured extreme pain during childbirth. The suffering must have been so immense that the mother named him 'pain'. Though none of this was his own fault, Jabez had to bear this tragic name for the rest of his life. Suffering had become his identity, a legacy passed down from his very birth.

From a human perspective, Jabez's life appears to be the most unfortunate. The prayer of Jabez is literally 'the prayer of pain'. How could a person born in such adversity and shame become the most honourable in the genealogy of the whole nation? The key to this transformation lies in his prayer. Only God could bring such transformation. In verse 10, Jabez entreated God,

> "Oh, that you would bless me and enlarge my territory! Let your hand be with me, and keep me from harm so that I will be free from pain."

An important note on the literary context

On the surface, the prayer seems to comprise four requests: blessing, expansion, God's presence, and protection. However, I must highlight a particular characteristic of ancient Hebrew literary practice which significantly impacts how we understand this prayer.

In ancient Hebrew writing, it was common to begin with a broad, general statement and gradually narrow it down, refining and clarifying it over the course of the writing. According to this Hebrew literary practice, these four requests in Jabez's prayer are essentially *one* request. The second clause explains the first clause, the third explains the second, and the fourth explains the third, making the prayer progressively clear.

In other words, Jabez was not asking for four separate things, but just one - God's blessing. How did he envision this blessing? He wanted it to come through the expansion of his territory. And how did he want this expansion to occur? The expansion would occur through God's hand (presence). In what manner did he wish for God's hand to be evident? It would be evident through God shielding him from harm and sparing him from pain.

Therefore, Jabez was making only one request with three levels of elaboration. He was carefully clarifying what he meant. Reading Jabez's prayer as one request has profound implications for how we apply the prayer in our lives today.

Let's examine the parts of the request one by one.

Understanding blessings and pain through Genesis 1–3

The first part of the prayer, "Oh, that you would bless me", may sound relatively straightforward. The word 'blessing' can carry all sorts of different meanings in different religious, social and cultural contexts. To understand what blessing means biblically, we must go all the way back to Genesis 1–3, the three chapters of the Bible that lay the foundation for many biblical concepts.

'Blessing' in the Bible can be traced back to Genesis 1 and 2, where God created the world and humans, and blessed them with fertility and sustenance. Interestingly, the term 'pain' first appears in the Bible subsequently in Genesis 3:16, in the context of God's judgment following the fall of humankind: "I will make your pains in childbearing very severe; with painful labour you will give birth to children."

While Genesis 1–2 narrates God's blessings on humankind, including the command to procreate abundantly, Genesis 3 narrates God's judgment. After God cursed the land and the Serpent, God did not curse Adam and Eve despite their rebellion. There was punishment for both Adam and Eve – one in toil while working on the land, the other in childbirth. Both are closely connected to procreation, and both are still rooted in God's blessings and provision. God never withdrew His blessings for them; In fact, God proclaimed their blessings would continue and they would still procreate abundantly. Only now, there would be additional factors – pain and toil.

Thus, we can see from the passage that pain is *not* a curse from God. The blessings God gave were not retracted in spite of human sin. One way of looking at pain is that it is a consequence of an exchange – the replacement of an original curse with a blessing. This does not imply that all pain is due to sin; rather, it means we shouldn't consider a person's life cursed simply because they experience pain and suffering. The Bible teaches that God's blessings are available to anyone in pain and suffering because it's God's will that we live a blessed life.

Jabez saw this clearly. In a situation where others might have felt cursed and believed they were doomed to a life of misery, Jabez never resigned himself to such a fate. He knew God was a God of blessing. Though Jabez had a painful beginning, his focus was not on his unfortunate origin. He looked up to a God who bestows blessings, and pain didn't hinder him from receiving these blessings. Hence, he boldly prayed for God to bless him, determined to break the supposed power of the curse. And what God loves doing most, and excels at, is breaking curses. Is there an aspect of your life where pain seems to persist like a curse? You can learn from Jabez, and actively ask God to bless you. If God desires to bless, we can undoubtedly seek blessings from Him.

Boundaries are not defined by pain but by God

From a human perspective, Jabez's life seemed hopeless, yet he knew the way out was to hold onto one truth: God is a blessing-giving God. How did he understand blessing? Jabez prayed: "Bless me *through* enlarging my territory!" This phrase seems a bit strange; expanding boundaries was not necessarily a good thing in the Old Testament. We must understand the context first in order to apply it correctly.

After the twelve tribes divided the land, everyone's territory was set. Moses's writings make it clear that land boundaries are unalterable, and one must not encroach on another's land (Deuteronomy 19:14, 27:17). The book of Proverbs also gives a similar directive (Proverbs 22:28, 23:10). The territory of each tribe, family and individual was already defined, and it couldn't be changed. Whose land was Jabez trying to expand into, then?

Jabez wasn't attempting to invade other tribes. He was seeking God's help to dispossess the Canaanites and inherit the land as God had promised (Exodus 34:24; Deuteronomy 19:8). The territories were divided, but the people hadn't possessed them yet as Canaan was inhabited by many enemies. To inherit the land, they had to drive out these enemies first and divide the land as per God's distribution. Many who failed to rely on God never succeeded and remained landless. Jabez's prayer wasn't about seizing more territory for himself (an unfortunate common misunderstanding of this prayer), but about asking God to help him so that his pain wouldn't impede him from receiving what was promised by God.

Jabez knew that God's blessing can surpass all the limitations in his life. To him, the pain wasn't an unbreakable spell but a surmountable obstacle. Very often, either consciously or unconsciously, we allow our suffering to limit us, confine our boundaries and define our calling. I have discussed the concept of a distorted self in previous chapters; those with a distorted self often feel lacking, believing they must use their own methods to compensate for deficiencies or to escape reality. Past traumas might make us fear and blame others or even God. Like many things in God's creation, God's calling allows room for growth and transformation, but we often unknowingly restrict God's calling.

There was once an experiment in raising sharks in small fish tanks. Such sharks stopped growing at eight inches. In larger tanks, they grew more, and in even bigger tanks or the ocean, they grew up to eight feet long. God's principle is similar. He designed sharks for the vast ocean where they can grow to large sizes. But limiting their space restricts growth. This applies to our growth as well. If we set limits, we won't be able to enjoy what God has promised.

Jabez's birth pain symbolised a life of suffering, hardships, obstacles, and constraints. He sought to overcome them. Note that this isn't about a sense of insatiability; it's about not letting these limits hinder our calling. Jabez wasn't surpassing his limitations by himself; he was relying solely on God. Many problems stem from relying on our methods for blessings. Some try to compensate with money, status, degrees and achievements, validating themselves through success. These methods may expand our personal boundaries in the short term, but like Jabez, we must rely on God's help alone and expand boundaries according to His will.

God's presence is the key to expanding our horizon

How does God bless us by expanding our territories? Through God's constant presence.

The original text of the prayer includes the word 'hand', as in "Your hand be with me." In the Old Testament, the notion of God's presence was often expressed in terms of God's hand being with His people. God's hand signified power.

Unlike Jabez, in the face of suffering that comes from our birth circumstances, our pain may drive us to think the pain is God's doing or another person's fault. Many of us would be tempted to blame God's hand rather than to seek it. Jabez's suffering certainly wasn't his or his mother's fault. He could have blamed his mother's painful experience on God. But rather than blaming God's hand, Jabez desired God's hand to be with him, empowering him to do His will. He never denied God's part in the suffering. His prayer essentially said, "You created this situation, so now I pray Your hand will empower me to overcome it."

God blesses, His powerful hand assists, so we never need to let pain, flaws or weaknesses hinder us. This theme resonates consistently throughout the Bible. The significance of Jabez's prayer lies in him letting God handle things. If you're weak or face difficulties, don't lose heart. As Paul learned, God's grace becomes most evident in our moments of weakness; His grace is always sufficient (2 Corinthians 12:9–10).

We often quote the verse, "My grace is sufficient for you." But have we truly lived it? Have we sought God's strength or leaned on our own? From now on, taste the grace of the Lord and seek His strength. Of course, it's according to His will, not ours.

When God calls us to do something, His hand will help us fulfil it. This is the definition of blessing in Scripture: God's presence will empower us to do His will. So, our prayer can be very straightforward: we can ask God to bless us by empowering us to live out His calling. The constraints in our lives are not setbacks; instead, they offer us a channel to witness and embrace God's overflowing grace.

Breaking the influence of the family tree while suffering remains

The last two lines are the focus of the prayer because they define the previous lines. How can God's presence help me? It is through "keeping me from harm so that I will be free from pain". At first glance, it sounds like a superficial prayer asking God to take my suffering away and make my path smooth.

This last part of Jabez's prayer is challenging to translate. The original text is very intriguing. It includes the words 'do' and 'hand'. A literal translation could be: "Do from evil, so not to pain me." Another possible translation is: "You do (work) [it] from evil, not to harm me." No translation can fully capture its essence.

The original text can also be understood as, "Your hand must work to prevent this suffering (evil) from harming me", or "May your hand be with me, may you act so that this hardship doesn't cause me pain." In other words, suffering still exists. The inherent pain won't change. Our lives are not free from suffering. However, God's grace can protect me from being destroyed by the pain, and I don't need to let this mark of pain prevent me from moving forward to live out God's calling. This seems to be the most fitting interpretation.

Instead of saying "God will remove this pain, and I will never feel pain again", Jabez acknowledged that suffering is an unchangeable fact. Jabez's goal wasn't to escape pain or hardship but to break free from their grip. Thus, while the pain still existed, it could no longer affect him. God's calling for him was to live with this suffering while living a blessed life and have God's hand to help him overcome the pain.

Many believers mistakenly believe that Christians should always be joyful due to the frequently quoted Bible verse: "Rejoice in the Lord always" (Philippians 4:4). Yet in the Bible, joy and suffering are never mutually exclusive. The Bible never teaches us to deny our pain or forget about it forever. We are empowered to face our pain and limitations, acknowledge their existence, and know that they can't harm us because God's hand is with us. This is true joy.

Praying the prayer of 'pain'

The genealogy describes Jabez as "more honourable than his brothers" (v. 9), highlighting his unique elevated status. What is the relationship between pain and honour? How could the most unfortunate person become the most honourable?

It turns out that all the shame and pain in our lives can be overcome. Pain not only doesn't need to become a curse, it can also be turned into honour. Jesus is the perfect example. As a descendant of Judah, Jesus Christ's life was filled with utmost suffering. No one knows pain as intimately as He does, for He was born destined for crucifixion.

Isaiah portrays the Messiah as a "suffering servant" whom others despised (Isaiah 52). The book of Philippians asserts that, due to Christ's humility and His sacrifice on the cross, God elevates Him to the highest place (Philippians 2:6–11). The Christian faith itself is marked by a symbol of pain and humiliation – the cross. Hence, pain cannot shake our relationship with God. Among all religions in the world, Christianity uniquely acknowledges that God Himself willingly endured suffering. Christianity is also the faith where death is the most powerless.

Jabez's prayer highlights God's grace and emphasises that God personally accomplishes everything despite pain and suffering. His prayer reveals a fact: even though we are limited by our weaknesses, this doesn't hinder us from fulfilling God's call. In fact, the weaker we are, the more God's grace is evident. The author's inclusion of these two verses about Jabez in the genealogy might have been intended to convey this message. He first points out that Jabez was the most honourable among many brothers, and then explains why he was the most honourable: because he prayed this prayer, and God granted his request.

Many of us are familiar with the Serenity Prayer: "God, grant me the serenity to accept the things I cannot change, the courage to change the things I can, and the wisdom to know the difference." Well, Jabez did not pray like that. The main point here isn't about finding out what can or cannot be changed, but whether you allow these things to hinder you and whether you know where your help truly comes from. Jabez's prayer tells us that we can bring all our pain, shame and limitations before God because God intends to bless us by helping us overcome. As long as this pain carries God's blessing, it no longer limits our pursuit of God's calling.

The most important thing is that Jabez didn't rely on his own methods or strength to make his name renowned in the genealogy. All the honour he received came directly from God who answered his prayer. Today, we can recommit ourselves with this prayer, not according to our own wishes, not relying on our own methods, but refocusing our gaze on the God who blesses, helps and expands our horizons so that we aren't held back by the pain that once defined our lives. Through this, we commit to faithfully living out God's calling in our lives.

20

The Canaanite Woman

Having examined the circumstances and prayer of a key Jewish ancestor in Judah's tribe in the Old Testament, we now turn our attention to a Gentile in the New Testament who, according to Jewish customs, should have had no connection to God's blessings whatsoever – the Canaanite woman (Matthew 15:21–28). Due to their non-Jewish lineage and socio-cultural status, Gentiles were traditionally regarded as outside the scope of God's grace. Yet the Bible has ample stories of Gentiles who received God's salvation in astounding ways as God empowered them to overcome boundaries that were seen as unbreakable.

Let's examine the story of the Canaanite woman. Like Jabez's prayer, this Gentile woman's prayer also earnestly sought God's help to transcend her limitations in seeking God's blessings:

21 Leaving that place, Jesus withdrew to the region of Tyre and Sidon. 22 A Canaanite woman from that vicinity came to him, crying out, "Lord, Son of David, have mercy on me! My daughter is demon-possessed and suffering terribly."

23 Jesus did not answer a word. So his disciples came to him and urged him, "Send her away, for she keeps crying out after us."

24 He answered, "I was sent only to the lost sheep of Israel."

> **25** The woman came and knelt before him. "Lord, help me!" she said.
>
> **26** He replied, "It is not right to take the children's bread and toss it to the dogs."
>
> **27** "Yes it is, Lord," she said. "Even the dogs eat the crumbs that fall from their master's table."
>
> **28** Then Jesus said to her, "Woman, you have great faith! Your request is granted." And her daughter was healed at that moment. (Matthew 15:21–28)

Indeed, this Scripture passage is not easy to interpret. Why did Jesus say the woman had great faith?

Prayer reflects how we view our relationship with God

Modern readers may be startled by how Jesus addressed the woman as a dog. However, to gain a comprehensive understanding of this story, it's crucial to understand it as it would have been understood by the people of that era. In Jesus's time, the most striking aspect in this story was *not* Jesus's use of the dog metaphor because it was a common expression used for Gentiles. Rather, the truly shocking aspect was the fact that a Greek woman from the vicinity of Tyre and Sidon addressed a Jewish rabbi as the "Son of David" and dared to seek his help in public with a supernatural problem. This would have been unheard of.

The title "Son of David", referring to the king of Israel and the promised Messiah, was mainly confined to the context of Judaism and had nothing to do with Gentiles. On the other hand, Tyre and Sidon were filled with pagan gods and superstitious practices, where Baal was predominantly worshipped. 1 Kings 16 records how Jezebel, the daughter of the king of Sidon, married an Israelite king, leading to the widespread worship of Baal in Israel, marking a dark period in Jewish history. How could someone from this region have possibly known who the Son of David was?

While most Jews didn't even accept Jesus as their Messiah, this Gentile woman not only openly acknowledged Jesus as the "Son of David", but also pleaded for his help to deliver her demon-afflicted daughter, thus displaying her faith in his spiritual authority as well. This is the first crucial step in prayer – to clearly recognise the true identity of the one we're speaking to and his authority.

Without a clear object of trust and worship, life easily descends into chaos and insecurity. Many people think they can rely solely on themselves, while others irrationally place their faith in anything they come across. Many Chinese people who have no religion often look to feng shui or other superstitious practices for reassurance. They can't find anything worthy of worship, but they need something to hold onto, so they look for alternative methods to secure luck and fortune. Life requires a solid foundation, and prayer is the expression of where our foundation lies. This woman acknowledged the foundation of her hope was Jesus.

When God is silent

Another puzzling aspect of this story is Jesus's apparent indifference to the woman. Jesus didn't attend to the woman initially, neither acknowledging her nor dismissing her despite her persistent cries. As described in verse 23: "Jesus did not answer a word." The God we believe in sometimes remains silent. Many believers have experienced this silence during prayer. God doesn't seem to be responding, our situations seem to remain unchanged, and prayers seem ineffective.

How do the disciples react? Verse 23 continues, "His disciples came to him and urged him, 'Send her away, for she keeps crying out after us.'" They wanted Jesus to either heal her daughter or send her away so she wouldn't bother them anymore. How did Jesus respond? He said:

> "I was sent only to the lost sheep of Israel." (v. 24)

Sent by the Father, Jesus's mission was to redeem the whole world, including the Gentiles, but his timeline was to first prioritise the Israelites in his ministry as the Good News would be shared with the Gentiles through them.

At times, we find it perplexing when it seems like God isn't attentive to our concerns. Our understanding is very limited. However, trusting God with childlike faith is sufficient. Like a child wholeheartedly trusting a father's promise, we must possess such unwavering faith. Though initially ignored, this woman remained steadfast in her belief that Jesus was her daughter's only hope. She persisted, kneeling before Him, pleading, "Lord, help me!" (v. 25).

Recognising who we are in God

Another perplexing part of this passage is, indeed, Jesus's use of the dog metaphor to refer to the foreign woman as a response to her desperate pleas. When she begged for mercy, Jesus said:

> "It is not right to take the children's bread and toss it to the dogs."
> (v. 26)

While his words may appear to have been cold and harsh, Jesus gave the woman a golden opportunity to display her faith and insights in front of the world, especially in front of the religious leaders who still had no clue about Jesus's identity and authority.

The woman had insight about who she was in God's kingdom and the divine help that was available to her. This is another fundamental element of faith-filled prayer – to recognise who we are in God's kingdom and His mercy.

When Jews referred to Gentiles as "dogs", they usually used the term for wild dogs. Here, Jesus deliberately used a different word which can be translated as "puppy" in modern English, meaning family dogs or small dogs. Jesus wasn't implying that these "dogs" (Gentiles) were not worthy of the gospel. Far from it. Both Jesus and the woman were in agreement that she was included in God's family. God's blessings are so abundant that even the leftovers are more than enough. This level of faith and understanding poses a striking contrast to the disciples in the story of the feeding of the five thousand, who try to disperse the people as they fear the food is not enough.

The woman displayed unwavering faith in her access to a merciful, abundant God. She fully understood that by God's mercy she could cross all the religious, social, cultural and racial barriers and confidently ask for God's help. She didn't take offence at Jesus's words; she understood that she was approaching God by God's mercy and not on her own merit. Jesus acknowledged her great faith and granted her request.

An interplay of contrasts

In this story, Jesus used two distinct animal analogical metaphors in response to two situations. The first imagery is found in verse 24, when Jesus answered the disciples, "I was sent only to the lost sheep of Israel." When Jesus said this, the woman hadn't approached him physically yet. She was merely shouting from a distance. He continued on his way, seemingly ignoring her, as if he was intending to leave quickly. The words in verse 24, therefore, are directed to the disciples, not the woman.

After the woman came and knelt before him (v. 25), Jesus presented a different imagery to her, "It is not right to take the children's bread and toss it to the dogs." The disparity in the animal images highlights a crucial message about approaching God with steadfast faith.

In the first instance, Jesus told his disciples that he came for the lost sheep of Israel. This is a pastoral scene, reminiscent of a parable Jesus once told about a shepherd who leads his flock to graze. When the shepherd realises one sheep is missing, he goes out searching for the lost one.

Imagine if you were the shepherd in Jesus's parable. While you're searching for your lost sheep, you encounter another stray animal along the way. Would you tend to the other animal and bring it home too? Of course not. Your mission is to rescue your own. A good shepherd focuses on his own sheep. Jesus used this imagery to teach his disciples that his primary focus now is to minister to his own people, the Israelites. Although other sheep are lost too, they weren't his immediate concern at the time. Jesus hoped that, upon hearing this, both the disciples and the Jews would cherish God's love and plan of redemption for them, for the Messiah had come specifically for them.

The four Gospels repeatedly highlight contrasts between the Jews (the insiders) who don't believe in Jesus and the Gentiles (the outsiders) who do. When addressing the Canaanite woman, Jesus didn't use the same sheep imagery. Instead, he used an everyday household scene to answer her: "It is not right to take the children's bread and toss it to the dogs."

The comparison between these two images is striking. In the first, the Shepherd, Jesus, seeks his own sheep in the wilderness, paying no attention to others. Verse 24 makes clear that these other sheep don't belong to Israel. In contrast, the second imagery presents a warm family scene, where everyone belongs, including the animals. The pets, the children's favourites, enjoy family food tossed to them.

In Jesus's second imagery, the status of the animal had changed completely. It had become part of the family, having a place at home to enjoy the abundance of food as the family dined together. Jesus's response set the stage for the woman's profound reply:

> "Yes it is, Lord," she said. "Even the dogs eat the crumbs that fall from their master's table." (v. 27)

These "crumbs" aren't referring to the tiny breadcrumbs we typically see today. The term refers to the pieces of bread used to clean dishes in ancient times. Given the absence of detergents, how did ancient households clean oily dishes? The wealthy would use pieces of bread to wipe their dishes and hands clean. Afterwards, they wouldn't eat this bread themselves, but give it to their pets. This bread would have been soaked with leftover food and even bits of meat, so it might have been quite delicious. In these households, when the family dined together, the dogs could gather near the table and enjoy their share.

On hearing Jesus's dog metaphor, the woman promptly picked up the hint and seized her opportunity to display her faith in God's boundless generosity. More importantly, she was fully aware of her own unworthiness, which explained why she wasn't offended by Jesus's analogy. She joyfully claimed her humble place in God's family. She knew she, even as a Gentile, was also included in God's abundant grace. When she acknowledged that even the leftovers were enough for her, she displayed her confidence in the vast magnitude of God's feast.

When we have full understanding and confidence in who God is and in our relationship with Him, we can transcend any limitations imposed by the world or by other people. Jesus rarely praises people for their great faith. He once noted that faith as small as a mustard seed is sufficient (Matthew 17:20), indicating that as long as the object of faith is correct, the magnitude of the faith isn't the issue. His praise for the woman wasn't just about her belief in Jesus. Rather, his praise was about her persistent hope despite all the social and cultural barriers she had to face. She firmly believed that her relationship with God wouldn't leave her empty-handed or deprive her of God's grace. That is what believing in God's promise "My grace is sufficient for you" looks like.

More biblical examples of overcoming barriers

What difficulties are hindering you from enjoying your share of the feast in God's kingdom? Beyond the stories of Jabez and the Canaanite woman, the Bible offers numerous examples of individuals transcending obstacles and limitations as they responded to God's calling. The book of Acts serves as a compelling illustration. More than just chronicling the spread of the gospel from Jerusalem, it serves as a testament to the apostles' journey of overcoming a myriad of challenges by the power of God.

Jesus had given the disciples a clear mandate: they were to spread the gospel starting in Jerusalem, then throughout Judea, into Samaria, and ultimately to the farthest corners of the known world (Acts 1:8). This command involved not only travelling through vast lands but also navigating the intricate landscapes of culture, religion, and politics. The geographical terrain posed the initial challenge, and in each new region they entered, the disciples encountered unique cultural and spiritual hurdles, as detailed in the chapters of Acts.

Acts chapter 2 brings us the story of Pentecost, a landmark event that celebrated the outpouring of the Holy Spirit and the miraculous gift of tongues. This gift was the breaking of specific linguistic barriers that were hindering the Jewish apostles from reaching the people groups God had called them to reach. The passage makes it clear that the tongues the apostles received were actual native languages of the Gentiles present at the scene (Acts 2:6, 8, 11) and were understood by the listeners present. While modern missionaries might benefit from language courses and translation tools, the apostles had no such aids. Their newfound ability to clearly articulate the gospel in other tongues was a divine intervention, enabling them to spread the gospel to Gentile regions at a speed previously impossible.

As the apostles pressed on, they encountered both physical threats and ideological confrontations. But God's way wasn't about eliminating every hindrance and paving a comfortable, smooth path for them. As adversities mounted, believers scattered, but this dispersion only furthered the reach of the gospel. The book of Acts reminds us that with God's help, no barrier is insurmountable when we set out to do what God has called us to do.

Re-evaluating all boundaries not set by God

In Acts chapter 8, we witness the disciples facing inevitable spiritual battles, starting with Simon the Sorcerer. The prevalent sorcery culture of the time posed significant psychological and spiritual barriers the disciples had to overcome in order to reach Simon. Remarkably, they succeeded in leading him to the Lord, baptising him, and bringing the gospel to other similar individuals.

The story of the Ethiopian eunuch also evidently demonstrates God's determination to save anyone who earnestly seeks Him While Philip's evangelising of the eunuch might appear straightforward, it was far from easy. Some sources suggest that the eunuchs of these countries were entirely castrated, making them physically incomplete and unable to be circumcised. Jewish customs dictated that these people didn't deserve God's grace. Today, these beliefs are being forgotten. However, back then, the disciples had to face a radical confrontation with numerous religious norms to baptise such individuals. Traditional thinking was deeply ingrained, and even the apostles once struggled with fully accepting the Gentiles. One can only imagine the breakthrough the Canaanite woman and the Ethiopian eunuch must have gone through.

These stories are also a sobering reminder for us to examine our own hearts and minds. While our calling is to share the Good News with people around us, do we impose additional constraints on people due to our own deeply ingrained beliefs? The most challenging hurdle to overcome is our personal biases. Some of us may be called to serve a particular group, such as prostitutes, marginalised youths or prisoners. Do we approach them with preconceptions? Would we place unnecessary hurdles on their path to seek God? For instance, if we're called to serve those with intellectual disabilities, what standards do we set for them to be baptised? Should we only baptise those who meet our personal standards that we have formed outside Scripture?

Many of our deeply held beliefs towards people around us need constant re-evaluation. Certain practices and traditions might need to be amended or even abandoned. It is imperative for us to reflect seriously to see whether our ministries are shaped by God or by our personal prejudices, and whether we have inadvertently created unnecessary stumbling blocks for others and ourselves.

God calls us to enter His kingdom as His beloved children. Although every generation and every believer have personal hurdles to overcome, God's grace is always sufficient. Bible stories like that of the Canaanite woman underscore a foundational truth in understanding God's calling: it has nothing to do with our credentials or lineage. God's calling challenges us to see beyond the conventional and to recognise that God's call is far-reaching, and, most importantly, available to all who seek Him with a genuine heart.

Even if the odds are stacked against us, once we readjust our perspectives and go forth with faith, nothing can hinder us from taking our rightful place in God's kingdom.

XI

Have you got what it takes?

The call to true discipleship

21

Jesus's response to 3 followers

mong the Bible's most significant and profound callings is the call to follow Jesus as his disciple. In this section, we will examine the essence of God's calling in the light of discipleship as taught by Jesus in the Gospels. Each Gospel paints a unique portrait of Jesus, and, in turn, offers a distinct perspective on what it means to be his disciple. In this chapter, we will look at Luke 9: 57-62, where Jesus provided a rich and illuminating definition of discipleship.

How does the Bible define 'follow'?

While Jesus appears to be highly exalted in Matthew's narratives, he appears approachable and down-to-earth in Luke's eyes. These depictions are not contradictory but highlight different aspects of Jesus. Luke focuses on the marginalised, giving special attention to sinners and women as they are often overlooked and despised. Jesus, as depicted by Luke, comes from humble beginnings, born in a manger and visited by lowly shepherds. He comes not to be a king but a servant. Yet Luke still has sobering teachings on what it means to truly follow Jesus:

> Whoever wants to be my disciple must deny themselves and take
> up their cross daily and follow me. (Luke 9:23)

This statement is also found in Matthew and Mark, but Luke dedicates almost an entire chapter to an explicit explanation of what it means. For Luke, the very essence of 'following' lies in "denying oneself", and in Luke 9:57–62, he provides some practical examples of how Jesus defined it:

> 57 As they were walking along the road, a man said to him, "I will follow you wherever you go."
>
> 58 Jesus replied, "Foxes have dens and birds have nests, but the Son of Man has nowhere to lay his head."
>
> 59 He said to another man, "Follow me."
> But he replied, "Lord, first let me go and bury my father."
>
> 60 Jesus said to him, "Let the dead bury their own dead, but you go and proclaim the kingdom of God."
>
> 61 Still another said, "I will follow you, Lord; but first let me go back and say goodbye to my family."
>
> 62 Jesus replied, "No-one who puts a hand to the plough and looks back is fit for service in the kingdom of God."

This passage contains more than meets the eye. It mentions three individuals' approaches to following the Lord and Jesus's reply to each of them. The first one said, "I will follow you wherever you go." His situation touches on the issue of home. The second one said, "Lord, first let me go and bury my father." His concern is the issue of family. The third one said, "I will follow you, Lord; but first let me go back and say goodbye to my family." He speaks about possessions and property. These three individuals and their circumstances all revolve around the concept of "home". Notice these three issues correspond to the three things God called Abram to leave behind when He promised to bless him (Genesis 12:1).

The issue of security

What do these three individuals represent? Let's start with the first. A man expressed his willingness to follow Jesus to the ends of the earth. Isn't that wonderful? But Jesus replied, "Foxes have dens and birds have nests, but the Son of Man has nowhere to lay his head" (Luke 9:58).

Foxes and birds have secure homes in their natural habitats. We all yearn for a secure home and a protective haven. However, the path of a disciple of Jesus is starkly different. This journey isn't anchored to earthly comforts or safety nets. Jesus makes it crystal clear that genuine discipleship demands a willing departure from these comforts.

Carrying your cross and denying yourself means you must let go of all your sources of security and rely on God alone. This is a recurring message throughout the Bible. Many chapters in this book tell us stories of how God's people cling to a false sense of security, only to miss out on God's calling and greater blessings God has prepared for them.

Learning to swim is a good analogy. Imagine someone who is terrified of water, but one day he witnesses a friend displaying amazing swimming skills. He admires the friend's abilities and desires to learn, so he says, "I want to learn whatever swimming techniques you teach me. Wherever you do, I will follow." The friend replies, "Sure! But there's one condition: you can't use a lifebuoy while learning to swim!"

In the same way, Jesus urged us to leave behind our lifebuoy when we decide to follow him. This doesn't mean that the path of discipleship is always full of danger and discomfort. That's not the point. Rather, it underscores the idea that real discipleship means giving up our self-made securities. The focus is not on risk but on the trust – the only way is to rely solely on Jesus.

Our homes symbolise our highest comfort. They are indeed a gift from God. Yet, God's call to us isn't merely about staying within the confines of our homes, but to step out like Abram when God calls, be willing to leave our comfort zones and seek His promises. This is daunting and requires great courage, but Jesus says clearly that following him demands this.

Luke's Gospel shows that Jesus's message especially resonates with the vulnerable. Those with the least often find it easier to let go. For the wealthy, there are too many ties that need severing. Yet Jesus's demands are reasonable. There's no point in learning to swim if you stay on the boat and refuse to get into the water.

The issue of priority

While Jesus addressed the issue of security in the first person, his focus is not as clear with the second person. Luke 9:59 shows that Jesus reached out and called this person to follow him, and the person's response was, "Lord, first let me go and bury my father." Jesus replied, "Let the dead bury their own dead, but you go and proclaim the kingdom of God" (v. 60).

Jesus seemed harsh, even heartless, especially when the man was only requesting to fulfil his filial duties before following him. Why would Jesus dissuade someone from burying a loved one?

Let's first understand the socio-cultural context regarding burial. In Jesus's times, Jewish mourning for a father was an elaborate affair, lasting several days, during which the sons would not leave the father's side at all. They would wait until the mourning period was over before resuming any other activity. If this man was walking along the road (v. 57), he likely wasn't in the process of mourning when he encountered Jesus. This means his father wasn't dead. He was just giving an excuse to delay his commitment.

Apart from looking at the social background, we can also see the original text doesn't imply that this man had just lost his father. What he was saying was, "I will follow you, Lord, but first let me go back and say goodbye to my family." His intention was to procrastinate until his father passed away before wholeheartedly following Jesus.

Jesus wasn't actually demanding that his disciples neglect their parents or ignore filial duties or funeral customs. Jesus was being witty here. When he said, "Let the dead bury their own dead", what he meant was: "The kingdom of God and the world of the dead are totally different realms. Following me is a matter of the eternal, divine realm. You don't need to let the affairs of the dead affect the affairs of the eternal kingdom. You just come and follow me." He essentially implored the man not to let temporal affairs hinder his pursuit of eternal life.

The reason given by this man, on the surface, seemed to be his responsibility to his family. In reality, it was a matter of priorities. For him, Jesus came second; someone else or other duties of this world occupied the top place of his list. He was thinking, "I'd like to follow you Jesus, but it's not your turn yet. Once I've settled other matters, I'll come join you." This is the reality of many people who claim to be Christians.

Jesus doesn't require us to neglect filial piety when we follow him; he is not asking us to be coldblooded. But Jesus reminds us that being his disciple means whole-hearted commitment. Sacrifices are unavoidable. It is not about whether or not we take care of our family, but about the priority in the choices we make and giving God's calling the highest priority. Take the example of missions: if God calls you to go overseas for missions, but your father wants you to stay and inherit the family business, then obeying your father's wishes would not be the right choice. Your choice reveals who your true family is and who your true Lord is.

When Jesus called this person to follow Him to proclaim the kingdom of God, he was making a comparison between the "kingdom" and "family", asserting that the kingdom of God should come before family. It may be necessary to forsake your family to follow the Lord.

Chinese people have a proverb: "Marry a chicken, follow the chicken; marry a dog, follow the dog." When a woman gets married, she should prioritise her husband's family over her original family. For example, she may not visit her own family as frequently as she had before marriage. It's not because she loves her own family less, but her identity has changed and her priorities have shifted. Sacrifices are inevitable in all committed relationships.

Professional athletes are another example. It's a tremendous honour to be selected to represent your country in the Olympics. You'd never hear a professional athlete say, "Let me wait until my father dies and his funeral is over before I compete." I know an athlete who willingly stayed away from home for an entire year only to be part of the Olympic Games opening ceremony. Such is the level of commitment required in the world of sports. If athletes show such devotion for earthly glory, shouldn't we give even greater commitment when we're called to follow the Lord?

The issue of not letting go

In the third person's case, Jesus addressed another matter. This person came forward on his own and said, "I will follow you, Lord; but first let me go back and say goodbye to my family" (v. 61). Although many modern translations use the word *family*, in the original text, there is no specific mention of *family*, only the term *home*. Essentially, what he meant was not saying goodbye to people, but parting with his possessions.

At first glance, there seems to be nothing wrong with this person's request. He said that once he had taken care of everything, he would follow Jesus. However, dealing with possessions can take a long time; it can take many days or months to complete a transaction for a property. The man was really saying, "I want to follow you, but there are still many things I need to handle at home. Once I have bid farewell to everything, I will follow you." There was reluctance in his heart. He still struggled to leave his old life behind.

Then Jesus suddenly began talking about ploughing a field. Most of us have never ploughed a field, so it's challenging to grasp the analogy Jesus used here. The strength of oxen is immense as they pull the plough, and if you want them to go where you want them to go, you must contend with them in strength. Otherwise, you risk losing control, and if you're not careful, you could even injure yourself. Therefore, when farmers use oxen to plough fields, they must look intently ahead and focus on controlling the oxen in front of them. Looking back and glancing around will only hinder them from steering the oxen. Essentially, Jesus was saying, "If you want to follow me but have your mind preoccupied with other things, you won't be able to do it at all."

This person had many attachments he couldn't let go of. If he had been willing, he would have already taken care of them and become a follower of

Jesus by this time. Perhaps he thought he could have the best of both worlds, but Jesus sternly pointed out to him that this would not be possible.

Many Christians who know God is calling them for full-time ministries have a similar mindset, wanting to arrange and settle everything related to their business, personal finances, relationships and so on before attending seminary. Does this mean that Jesus thinks it is wrong to make some preparations before following Him? Jesus's response showed that he doesn't mean that at all. What did Jesus say? He said, "No-one who puts a hand to the plough and looks back is fit for service in the kingdom of God" (v. 62). To put a hand on the plough and look back means that this person is still attached to his possessions and is unable to let go. This is unacceptable.

Many believers know what God is calling them to do, such as leaving their beloved job or sacrificing certain things, but they just can't bring themselves to do it. They keep bargaining with God, saying, "Please let me just keep a few things. Give me a little more time to prepare." In verse 62, Jesus bluntly pointed out these people are not "fit for service in the kingdom of God." It's like the example of an athlete: if your country values you and selects you to be a full-time athlete for the national team, but you say you only want to be a part-time amateur, then you disqualify yourself.

Letting go is an ongoing process. In human terms, it's not something that can be achieved all at once. We must be aware that being a disciple involves constantly letting go and surrendering. God commands us to love Him with all our hearts, all our souls, all our minds and all our strength. He asks us to love Him far more than we love our parents and says that obedience is better than sacrifice. All these commands emphasise that God must take the first place in our life. We cannot allow any other love to replace or compete with the love we have for Him.

Money is a prime example of something that people cling tightly to, unable to let go. However, Jesus teaches that we cannot serve both God and Mammon (money). Consider the parable of the shrewd manager in Luke 16:1–13. The steward was praised by Jesus for his shrewdness (Luke 16:1–13) because before leaving his job, he took the opportunity to use his master's money to pave the way for his future. He knew that the money wouldn't last and didn't belong to him anyway, but it could be leveraged for enduring benefits in the future. He did exactly that, and that's where his cleverness lay.

Jesus pointed out that even the people of the world know how to use temporary things to serve themselves, so why weren't his disciples seizing the same opportunities to let go of their temporal resources in exchange for eternal wealth?

Three pictures, One Lord

In this passage, three distinct pictures are presented. The first one focuses on assurance, addressing the issue of faith. Many people want to follow the Lord, but they also seek to maintain their own sources of assurance, certainty, and security. However, Jesus says, "No. Rely on me by faith alone." The second one concerns priority, illustrating the concept of faithfulness. It poses the question: do you prioritise family or God's kingdom? The third one touches on attachment, dealing with one's love for God. Jesus was asking the same question he asked Peter: "Do you love me more than these?" Or do you still have attachments and lingering affections?

These three scenarios appear in a sequence. To understand the author's intentions, we can start by comparing them. We have already compared the dialogues of the three individuals with Jesus which bring forth three requirements of discipleship. Now, let's review the introductions of the three individuals. Luke's arrangement is noteworthy as it not only reveals varying levels of willingness to follow Jesus but also demonstrates three levels of understanding about discipleship:

The first person came on his own, probably out of an impulsive interest, not expecting that following Jesus would be so serious. So, Jesus instructed him to go back and think it through, leading him to realise that following the Lord demanded that he give up his own security. The second person was called by Jesus. Once he heard the call, he immediately considered that there were many things to think about. He asked Jesus to let him first fulfil his family responsibilities. The third person also came on his own, but he had already considered it carefully, and said, "I still have some matters to attend to, but after thinking it through, I still want to follow You."

The story presents a progressive arrangement: the first one hadn't considered the cost at all; the second one considered it only after Jesus called him; and the third one had considered before coming. Look closely at Jesus's responses. Notably, only the third one was rejected. Jesus didn't reject the first two. What Jesus was effectively saying was, to the first one: "Do you know that following me means leaving behind your sense of security? If you know that, you can come." To the second one: "Earthly matters shouldn't hinder you from pursuing God's kingdom. You just come follow me now." But to the third one, Jesus's message was much sterner: "Do you think you can follow me without giving up other things? You're not fit for this kingdom!" We can imagine once the third man goes back, he will not return because he cannot bear to leave his things.

Jesus's responses to the three individuals also teach us different lessons in today's context. The first response teaches us that following the Lord requires being prepared to adapt to changes at any time and to step out of one's comfort zone. This underscores the importance of faith, a lesson that every disciple, regardless of their profession, must embrace. The second response is an important guide to Christians who may be grappling with conflicting priorities in their lives. But once we understand that the concerns of this world and the kingdom of God exist in separate realms, they no longer hinder us from following Jesus wholeheartedly. This highlights the significance of faithfulness. The third response delivers a harsh lesson for Christians who still cling to attachments from their old lives and think that following the Lord doesn't require giving up everything. This is, in fact, the most dangerous. This speaks of genuine love and highlights the fact that true discipleship is total devotion.

Three individuals, three situations, Luke presents them in plain language, illustrating that following Jesus involves different costs and challenges. The essence of following the Lord lies in our sacrificial commitment in all these three areas. Luke often highlights the concept of self-denial in Jesus's teachings, and this is precisely the kind of self-denial Jesus was talking about.

22

Jesus's response to 3 temptations

How did Jesus himself live out his commitment and obedience to what he was called to do on earth? We can find the answer in the very first thing he did when he started his ministry. Interestingly, his way of kickstarting his ministry was drastically different from what we might expect in today's context. Many of us might anticipate a ministry leader to dive into a whirlwind of public speeches, promotional campaigns or a series of spectacular miracles. Not Jesus. The Bible tells us that just before he officially began his public appearance,

> Jesus was led by the Spirit into the wilderness to be tempted by the devil. (Matthew 4:1)

What a surprising way to start ministry! However, there shouldn't be any surprise. Answering God's calling with obedience always entails overcoming trials and resisting the enemy's schemes. Jesus's tackling of the devil's three temptations provides us with an immensely valuable role model in our journey of living out God's calling.

How exactly did the devil tempt Jesus? And how did Jesus navigate the challenges? The key to grasping the devil's motives lies in understanding Jesus's steadfast responses in Matthew 4:2–11:

2 After fasting for forty days and forty nights, he was hungry. **3** The tempter came to him and said, "If you are the Son of God, tell these stones to become bread."

4 Jesus answered, "It is written: 'Man shall not live on bread alone, but on every word that comes from the mouth of God.'"

5 Then the devil took him to the holy city and had him stand on the highest point of the temple. **6** "If you are the Son of God," he said, "throw yourself down. For it is written: "'He will command his angels concerning you, and they will lift you up in their hands, so that you will not strike your foot against a stone.'"

7 Jesus answered him, "It is also written: 'Do not put the Lord your God to the test.'"

8 Again, the devil took him to a very high mountain and showed him all the kingdoms of the world and their splendour. **9** "All this I will give you," he said, "if you will bow down and worship me."

10 Jesus said to him, "Away from me, Satan! For it is written: 'Worship the Lord your God, and serve him only.'"

11 Then the devil left him, and angels came and attended him.

Observe the settings of each temptation: They went from the wilderness to the holy city and finally ascended a high mountain. This progression symbolises the increasing intensity of the trials. But first, let's look at a common thread that runs through these three temptations – Jesus responded with Scripture every time. Apart from quoting Scripture, he didn't say much at all. Furthermore, notice all three passages quoted by Jesus come from Deuteronomy, a book that chronicles the period when God's people were tested in the wilderness. This consistency carries great significance.

Living on God's Word

The first temptation saw the devil urging Jesus to turn stones into bread. This might seem like a harmless suggestion when one is famished. Yet, Jesus responded, "It is written: 'Man shall not live on bread alone, but on every word that comes from the mouth of God'" (v. 4). This statement originates from Deuteronomy 8:3, which refers to the time when the Israelites were tested in the wilderness. What was the context? And what was this test intended to assess?

The Israelites survived in the wilderness for forty years. I would say this was the greatest miracle in the Old Testament (while the New Testament's greatest miracle is Jesus's resurrection). For the millions of people camping in a vast, arid land, finding a drop of drinking water would be challenging enough, let alone finding food. And it might have been hard enough for a day, but they survived forty years. In fact, some Jewish scholars today do not believe that such events ever occurred due to its impossibility. Sceptics have proposed many theories, such as claiming there was no Exodus or that the Torah was written much later as a national myth. In short, they try to deny this miracle.

This test was indeed severe, which explains why the Israelites were so disobedient. It's not easy to believe that food and water are accessible to you in the wilderness, especially when you're with millions of people in the same situation. Survival was the most pressing concern for this large group of people.

In such a situation, God said, "Man does not live on bread alone but on every word that comes from the mouth of the Lord" (Deut. 8:3). In the life-and-death circumstances, God pointed out to the people that what they needed was obedience – heeding God's Word and keeping the covenant He had established with them. He would then protect them and provide them with the utmost reliable security. This is what the test was about.

When we examine how Jesus replied to the devil, we see that each of Jesus's answers contains an important word. In the first test, the word is 'on' (or sometimes translated as 'by'); in the Chinese Bible it is translated as 'depend' or 'rely'. What you depend on shows what you truly believe in. Jesus's answer presents a contrast: in order to live, we do not depend on food alone but on God's word.

How did Jesus pass this test? By relying on the Word of God. In the wilderness, the Israelites, no longer having to labour for the Egyptians to earn a living, had to obey God's word and rely on the Lord. Similarly, Jesus had to obey God's Word. Therefore, he firmly rejected the devil's words.

This leads to another question: what's wrong with turning stones into bread? Pay attention to how the devil phrased this temptation. In verse 3, the devil started by saying, "If you are the Son of God . . . ", implying that since Jesus was the Son of God, he could do anything, including turning stones into bread. Then he wouldn't have to suffer from hunger. Turning stones into food is not wrong in itself. Jesus indeed had the power to do it, but he refused to do so at this moment. He demonstrated that being the Son of God doesn't mean he doesn't need to obey. He was effectively saying, "No. *Even though* I am the Son of God, I will still obey my Father God to the end."

Acknowledging who is really in charge

The second temptation is not easily understood. In ancient times, the temple was the highest structure. The devil took Jesus to the pinnacle of the temple and suggested that if Jesus was the Son of God, he could jump from the top of the temple. The devil's reasoning was, "For it is written: 'He will command his angels concerning you, and they will lift you up in their hands'" (Matt. 4:6).

Many readers think that this temptation aimed to lure Jesus into vanity and to showing off his supernatural abilities. However, Jesus's response, "Do not put the Lord your God to the test", seems to address much more than that. While the true intention behind this temptation may not be easy to grasp by modern readers, the Jewish audience of that time could readily understand it within the historical context of the Scripture quoted by Jesus. It is drawn from Deuteronomy 6:16, "Do not put the Lord your God to the test as you did at Massah."

How did the Israelites test God at Massah? The people arrived at Rephidim and found no water, so they grumbled against Moses (Exodus 17:1). Moses asked them, "Why do you quarrel with me? Why do you put the Lord to the test?" (Exodus 17:2). But the people persisted and demanded water no matter what. Verse 3 says, "But the people were thirsty for water there, and they grumbled against Moses. They said, 'Why did you bring us up out of Egypt to make us and our children and livestock die of thirst?'"

Where did the Israelites go wrong at Massah? It might not be evident just by looking at Exodus 17 alone. However, if we look back at chapters 15 and 16, the picture becomes clearer. First, they complained about the bitter water at Marah, and Moses made the water fit for drinking (Exodus 15:22–25). Then, when they lacked food, they complained about the lack of meat (Exodus 16:1–30; Numbers 11:4–32). Now, at Massah, they grumbled again because of the lack of water. The root of the people's problem was that they wanted God to fulfil all their desires and continuously tested the limits of what God would provide.

The important word Jesus used in the second temptation is the verb 'to test.' This is the key to Jesus's response to the devil: "Do not put the Lord your God to the test." Deuteronomy 8:2 makes it clear: "Remember how the Lord your God led you all the way in the wilderness these forty years, to humble and test you in order to know what was in your heart, whether or not you would keep his commands."

The crux of the problem: who obeys whom?

The second temptation may not seem directly related to the previous one, but it is. The contrast between Jesus and the devil is evident in the first temptation – who to trust: food or God's word? The second temptation also has a contrast – should man obey God or should God obey man? At that time, people would immediately understand that this was a question of authority because they were familiar with the story in Deuteronomy 8.

It's easier to understand this through the lens of parenting experiences.

When parents teach their children, they train them to listen and obey. Yet, if children turn around and expect the parents to obey them, what would happen? Just like a child's constant nagging, testing the parents' limits, the Israelites also tried to manipulate God to give in to their demands. Originally, it was the people being tested by God to see if they would obey. However, over time, they tried to reverse the roles. When Moses asked the Israelites why they tested God, that was what he meant.

While the first temptation addressed the issue of needs, this one addressed the issue of demands. This time, it was not about reliance but about obedience. God brought the Israelites all the way from Egypt to the wilderness, and now, they were insinuating, "If You don't comply with us, we won't want You." These resentful words echoed repeatedly, as if they were testing whether God would truly submit to their desires.

Adversity reveals our true colours – do we obey God, or do we want God to obey us? When things go awry, and God does not comply with our wishes, we are prone to complain. Complaining is human nature; seeking help is natural. The problem arises when we say to God, "Since you didn't give me what I asked for, I don't want you anymore!" This mirrors the devil's attempt to deceive Jesus in a similar manner. Jesus's response, "Do not put the Lord your God to the test," underscores the importance of not trying to take God's position. Do we test God, or is it God who tests us? God is the one we should obey and serve, not the other way around.

Where does your heart truly lie?

Finally, the devil took Jesus to a high mountain from where they could overlook all the nations of the world. All the splendour and wealth of the world were displayed before him. The devil said that if Jesus bowed down and worshipped him, he would gain all of it. Jesus's response, however, was, "Away from me, Satan! For it is written: 'Worship the Lord your God and serve him only'" (v. 10).

The important word Jesus used here is the word 'worship'. As in the previous two situations, Jesus's response here immediately posed a contrast:

worshiping the devil, who promised to give you the entire world, versus worshiping God, who commanded you to go to the cross. Prior to this, Jesus's faith and loyalty had been tested, and now this test targets his love. When Satan showed Jesus the world and tested whom he would choose to worship, Jesus unequivocally chose to worship God.

The devil's method of tempting is worth noting. There are similarities between the three temptations, but there is one striking difference. In the first two temptations, the devil began by saying, "If you are the Son of God", but he didn't mention it in the third temptation. Why is that? Because this time, Satan wanted Jesus to give up being the Son of God.

The fact that Jesus is the Son of God carries two significant meanings. First, this is a message that Matthew strongly emphasised. In Matthew 2, the infant Jesus was sought by Herod who wanted to kill him. Joseph hurriedly took him and Mary to Egypt, fulfilling the prophecy, "Out of Egypt I called my son" (Matthew 2:15). The Jews had always regarded Israel as the Son of God, and now Jesus, *the* Son of God, identified completely with them.

This identification is important. Jesus faced on our behalf the same trials humanity needed to face: the same wilderness, the same challenges and temptations. Once it was forty years, now it was forty days. Just as the Israelites underwent trials, so did the Son of God. The teachings given to the Israelites by Moses in Deuteronomy (6:13) are now used by Jesus in response to the same events – a deliberate arrangement for comparison. Forty years of wandering in the wilderness represents our life journey, and the Son of God also personally went through it, fully identifying with humanity.

An identity that defines obedience

Second, according to Hebrews 12:6–8, every son will experience being tested:

> **6** Because the Lord disciplines the one he loves, and he chastens everyone he accepts as his son.
>
> **7** Endure hardship as discipline; God is treating you as his children. For what children are not disciplined by their father?
> **8** If you are not disciplined – and everyone undergoes discipline – then you are not legitimate, not true sons and daughters at all.

The "discipline" mentioned here doesn't refer to the kind where a son does something wrong and the father punishes him. Instead, it refers to training, refining, and the shaping of character. In the past, having many sons was common, and among them, there might be illegitimate ones with no official status. Only the favoured son whom the father treasured most would inherit the estate. The father would specially train him and invest much effort in bringing him up. The illegitimate sons would not be subjected to such training.

Jesus was no exception. The book of Hebrews tells us that precisely because Jesus is the Son of God, He needed to go through trials through obedience (Hebrews 5:8-10). Previously, Satan tried to tempt Jesus to go against this principle, using the opening line "If you are the Son of God". The implication was, "Since you are the Son of God, you can do whatever you want." This time, the devil was asking, "Why not be *my* son? Your future is the cross, with only one dead end. If you become my son, you won't have to go through all this hardship. I can give you everything you desire."

Again, Jesus immediately rejected Satan's suggestion and stated he would only worship and obey God alone.

Three temptations covering three levels of obedience

As mentioned earlier, the three temptations progressively increase in severity – from the wilderness to the top of the temple and then to the highest mountain. The three also point to three different real-life situations, testing our faith, loyalty, and love respectively. This can be a symbolic representation, indicating that the temptations Satan presented become increasingly attractive. At the same time, we also see Satan's sophisticated methods. Satan didn't openly and brazenly tempt Jesus from the beginning. Instead, it was a gradual escalation, becoming more cunning, which is the most dangerous aspect.

Why is that? The first temptation seems harmless – turning stones into bread when hungry, which, in itself, isn't problematic. When your survival is uncertain, and your life seems to have no means to sustain it, can you still trust God and hold onto your faith?

The second temptation, using Scripture to justify an action, doesn't seem too irreverent either. Satan didn't begin with a direct threat but with an ambiguous lie. It progressed step by step, making the initial actions appear harmless, like coaxing someone with their best interests in mind. When God doesn't conform to your desires, can you still remain loyal to Him, being faithful without wavering?

Lastly, the third temptation presents a beautiful prospect: when wealth, fame, and the things you desire the most are all promised to you if you give up your identity in God, can you resist the temptation? What is it that you truly pursue? What is your deepest longing and greatest desire?

Satan is incredibly clever. When he first tempted Eve in Genesis 3, he appeared as a serpent, not a large vicious beast. He came to Eve with sweet words, making Eve doubt God's words and love, gradually making her feel like God was not on her side. Satan knows very well that people are more likely to fall for ambiguous, seemingly reasonable lies. So, we must be careful; the devil is gradually luring people and becoming bolder. Many people fall, such as into extramarital affairs, because in the beginning they don't feel anything is wrong. As a result, they sink deeper and can't extricate themselves.

Jesus's method of dealing with temptation was to not only counter each temptation with God's Word, but to do so in a way that exposed the lure of the temptation and directly opposed it. This shows how we all have a choice to make: relying on food or relying on God's words; obeying God or expecting God to obey us; worshipping the devil or worshipping God. Each time, Jesus chose God.

Run to the Heavenly Father and be firmly rooted in His Word

The book of James teaches that whenever we face temptation, we should immediately run to God to draw near to Him, and He will draw near to us; and if we resist the devil, he will flee from us (James 4:7–8). This was precisely Jesus's method. We are defenceless against the devil without God. It's like taking three-year-old children to the street. Would you teach the toddlers, "If a stranger talks to you, you should reply like this . . ."? Of course not. You would teach them not to accept anything from strangers and to immediately run back to their parents. You wouldn't teach them how to negotiate with strangers; they wouldn't have the ability to handle it.

Facing temptation is an inescapable aspect of life. When facing temptation, we must immediately distance ourselves from it and run to God, not try to confront it ourselves. If we allow ourselves to hear the devil's enticing words, lingering precariously at the edge of temptation, the risk of being deceived is very high. We must remember that, while our spirit might be willing, our human frailty can be easily outmanoeuvred by Satan's cunning schemes. Jesus confronted temptation not through his own will, but by grounding himself firmly in God's Word. This strategy is our only hope, our surest sanctuary, because Satan can't beat God's Word.

The three temptations Jesus faced are reflective of the range of challenges we all confront while taking up God's calling for our lives, whatever our calling may be. Jesus, embodying the human experience, navigated each trial and emerged triumphant in every instance at the start of his mission on earth. We are called and empowered to do the same.

XII

Are you ready to go all the way?

The call to surrender all

23

Jesus in the Transfiguration

I n our journey of understanding God's calling and personal transformation, it's crucial to recognise not only who we are in God's eyes but also that God has called us to know and experience Him intimately. However, many Christians mistakenly believe that supernatural encounters or heightened spiritual experiences are necessary for a deeper connection with God. The pursuit of this approach, while commonly found in other pagan religions, is not found in the Bible. This chapter will explore a particular supernatural event Jesus shared with three of his disciples – the story of Jesus's transfiguration – to learn more about the biblical approach to spiritual growth and guidance.

A once-in-a-lifetime spiritual encounter

What is the ultimate spiritual experience? The account of Jesus's transfiguration in Luke 9:28–36 provides a profound answer:

> 28 About eight days after Jesus said this, he took Peter, John and James with him and went up onto a mountain to pray. 29 As he was praying, the appearance of his face changed, and his clothes became as bright as a flash of lightning. 30 Two men, Moses and Elijah,

appeared in glorious splendour, talking with Jesus. [31] They spoke about his departure, which he was about to bring to fulfilment at Jerusalem. [32] Peter and his companions were very sleepy, but when they became fully awake, they saw his glory and the two men standing with him. [33] As the men were leaving Jesus, Peter said to him, "Master, it is good for us to be here. Let us put up three shelters – one for you, one for Moses and one for Elijah." (He did not know what he was saying.)

[34] While he was speaking, a cloud appeared and covered them, and they were afraid as they entered the cloud. [35] A voice came from the cloud, saying, "This is my Son, whom I have chosen; listen to him." [36] When the voice had spoken, they found that Jesus was alone. The disciples kept this to themselves and did not tell anyone at that time what they had seen.

This event was the first time Jesus had visually and supernaturally revealed his divinity to his disciples. It was also the last time. This extraordinary experience was only granted to three of the disciples: Peter, John and James. The other nine weren't included at all.

Many Christians believe we may experience such spectacular encounters with God as long as we have enough faith or pray in a special way. Indeed, Jesus and the disciples were praying, but the passage doesn't mention a special prayer, nor is the content of Jesus's prayers mentioned. It was their routine to climb up a mountain to pray. Only this time, Jesus's appearance dramatically changed, radiating in dazzling light.

Had the three disciples done something special to make this happen or to gain access to this supernatural scene? Evidently not. The passage emphasises that the disciples were "sleepy" and pretty much slept through most of the event (v. 32). By the time they were fully awake, the transfiguration had happened already, as if God deliberately hid the process from them. When Jesus was about to return to his original form, a cloud overshadowed everyone, so the disciples remained clueless about how the change took place.

Uncontrollable and irreproducible

All spiritual experiences are initiated by God in His timing. This is a crucial understanding. God is not known to us unless He chooses to reveal Himself to us. Peter, in his eagerness to hold onto the spectacular moment, impulsively suggested building three shelters to keep Moses, Elijah, and the transformed Jesus with them. Luke's account poignantly demonstrates that the disciples couldn't comprehend, let alone retain, this heightened spiritual experience. An encounter with God, even when documented, might capture only a fraction of the actual experience.

Peter's failed attempt to capture the trio reveals a fundamental truth: experiences of God can't be retained, replicated or manipulated. No spiritual practice can guarantee to generate a certain spiritual experience because experiencing God's presence is not the outcome of a formula or method.

Spiritual disciplines like reading the Bible, praying, and meditating Scripture are all beneficial. These are channels that help us open up our hearts and draw closer to God. They help filter out distractions and prepare our hearts to receive and understand God's Word. However, it's essential to understand the roles these disciplines play in our relationship with God. It's a dangerous fallacy to believe that a particular spiritual practice, prayer or action will generate specific spiritual experiences we desire, as if there's a way to manipulate the Holy Spirit. Not even the most seasoned spiritual mentors, pastors or theologians can dictate how and when they experience God's presence.

The relationship we have with God is a living and dynamic relationship, and it's beyond our ability to manipulate or control. It's pointless trying to generate a certain experience for ourselves. All aspects of our encounter with God, including the nature and timing, remain under God's sovereignty.

No retainable images, only Word

What else did the disciples witness apart from Jesus radiating with a glorious light? Verse 35 mentions, "A voice from the cloud, saying . . ." This is also a crucial concept highlighted in the Old Testament: listening to the Word of God is always more important than seeing visual images or signs. Deuteronomy chapter 4 clearly speaks of this.

Deuteronomy recounts how after the Israelites spent a generation wandering in the wilderness, and just before they were to enter Canaan, Moses reminded them of his experience on Mount Sinai and reiterated the laws given by God on the mountain. Only Moses was allowed to ascend Mount Sinai, marking his closest encounter with God and God's first revelation and the giving of His laws to the nation of Israel. What did the people see while waiting at the base of the mountain? Nothing. Deuteronomy 4:11 states:

> You came near and stood at the foot of the mountain while it blazed
> with fire to the very heavens, with black clouds and deep darkness.

Like the scene of Jesus's transfiguration, many of the details were veiled from the people. In fact, God's splendour is so intense that if He had allowed anyone to see Him, it would have been fatal. The point isn't to scare us, but to assert that we humans simply cannot behold God. Deuteronomy 4:12 clarifies:

> Then the Lord spoke to you out of the fire. You heard the sound
> of words but saw no form; there was only a voice.

The people could only hear God's commandments but saw nothing with their eyes. The primary reason is outlined in the same chapter, verses 15–19:

15 You saw no form of any kind the day the Lord spoke to you at Horeb out of the fire. Therefore watch yourselves very carefully, **16** so that you do not become corrupt and make for yourselves an idol, an image of any shape, whether formed like a man or a woman, **17** or like any animal on earth or any bird that flies in the air, **18** or like any creature that moves along the ground or any fish in the waters below. **19** And when you look up to the sky and see the sun, the moon and the stars – all the heavenly array – do not be enticed into bowing down to them and worshipping things the Lord your God has apportioned to all the nations under heaven.

Why didn't God allow the people to see His form? This was to prevent them from carving idols for worship after seeing Him. This is how pagan religions work. Such idols, on the surface, might represent God, but they're actually human tools for controlling God. We are all created in God's image, but our rebellious nature prompts us to create God in our own image instead. With these self-created images, we can choose to worship the version of God that suits our expectations and we can worship Him as we please. In essence, it's about exerting control, much like Peter's attempt to capture the transcendent Jesus, trying to keep him in a form he could control and experience. Yet the second commandment commands us:

You shall not make for yourself an image in the form of anything in heaven above or on the earth beneath or in the waters below. (Exodus 20:4)

It's a temptation many of us face. We unknowingly create our own concept of God, our own idea of Jesus, and our own version of the Holy Spirit. Since God is so good, we seek tangible representations of Him, hoping for a firmer grasp of the intangible so that we can experience God whenever and however we want. We're all prone to do this, and Peter was no exception.

This desire might not originate out of disrespect towards God, but God will never allow it. What can we do instead? Be rooted firmly in God's living Word alone, His revelation about Himself.

We can't see God's face, but we can indeed read His Word. This was the case when God delivered the laws to the Israelites through Moses, and it was the same during Jesus's transfiguration. Luke 9:35 records a voice from the cloud saying, "This is my Son, whom I have chosen." The command that follows is, "Listen to him." Listening and obedience are the key to our walk with God.

Apart from the fact that the disciples didn't actually see much of the transformation process, another notable point in the story is that they witness a conversation between Elijah, Moses and Jesus (Luke 9:30–31). Elijah represents the prophets, and Moses the law. Together, they symbolise the Word of God, and they both point towards Christ. Deuteronomy mentions God raising a prophet like Moses (Deut. 18:7–18; see Acts 3:22), referring to Jesus Christ. Similarly, Elijah would come to pave the way for the Messiah. Both the Torah and the Prophetic Books speak of the coming of the Messiah, hence the voice saying, "This is my Son, whom I have chosen; listen to him" (v. 35).

Seeing Moses and Elijah together affirming Jesus was indeed significant. However, more important than their appearance was the content of their conversation. What were they discussing? The passage points out clearly their dialogue was about:

> [Jesus's] departure, which he was about to bring to fulfilment at Jerusalem (v. 31).

The voice said, "Listen to him", but listen to what? The disciples heard a conversation, and while the exact words aren't recorded, the message was clear: Jesus would die as a fulfilment of the Law and God's prophecies.

Obedient to death – even death on a cross

So, the whole dramatic transfiguration on the mountain was essentially a confirmation of what the disciples had been struggling to believe: Jesus's imminent death. This is not how we usually picture spiritual experiences. Aren't these experiences meant to make us feel elated, happy and 'high'?

The purpose of the transfiguration was to serve as a continuation and confirmation of Jesus's prior prophecy that he would suffer, die and rise again, and a call for his disciples to deny themselves and take up their crosses to follow Him (Luke 9:23). About eight days after the prophecy, the disciples witnessed his transfiguration on the mountain. At the heart of Jesus's transfiguration is the call for humility, obedience and self-denial.

Let us ask ourselves what we are pursuing in our walk with God? Our spiritual journeys aren't meant to be a pursuit of exciting experiences, but rather, to humbly carry the cross and follow Jesus in obedience. It's not about 'self-gain' but rather 'self-denial'. The conversation between Moses, Elijah, and Jesus on the mountain signifies how everything in the Old Testament pointed to the Messiah's sacrifice in Jerusalem, just as Jesus had foretold.

We don't need to envy Peter, John and James for witnessing Jesus's transfiguration. It may seem desirable to have transcendent experiences. However, while spiritual highs are exhilarating, they easily lead us to feel proud and superior to others. These transcendent moments, then, can be dangerous in our walk with God.

Many things can hinder our closeness to God – pride, disbelief or anxiety, for example. These barriers prevent us from hearing God's voice and approaching Him. When are we closest to God? It's often when we are at our lowest, feeling the most inadequate, and desperately holding onto Him. No wonder some people say spirituality isn't a continuous ascent but the continuous letting go of what isn't of God.

This is not to say that emotionally charged spiritual experiences are bad. In fact, the presence or absence of these spiritual highs isn't the main concern. Scripture never calls us to seek thrilling supernatural experiences. What does God wish to see in His people? Or rather, who is worthy of entering

God's temple? It's those who recognise their inadequacies and unworthiness. God is close to those who are broken in spirit, not necessarily those 'high' in spirit. Letting go of pride, personal desires, self-righteousness, and relying solely on God is the spiritual state we truly need.

Have you ever looked at the transfiguration story in the context of the whole chapter of Luke 9? Right after they descended the mountain, Jesus was reunited with the other nine disciples, only to find they had been struggling with casting out a demon (9:37–45). Soon after, the disciples argued among themselves about who would be the greatest (9:46–49); then upon facing rejection from the Samaritans, the disciples wondered if they should call fire from heaven to destroy them (9:52–55). Sadly, right after the experience of Jesus's transfiguration, the disciples were still blinded by their own arrogance and self-centredness. They failed to grasp Jesus's call to carry their cross to follow Jesus. Supernatural experiences don't necessarily draw us closer to God.

At the end of chapter 9, we see that three individuals who wished to follow Jesus are sternly instructed by Jesus to let go of something (see Chapter 21 of this book). The story of the transfiguration is sandwiched between all these teachings about self-denial. This was what the transfiguration was truly about.

Obedience and letting go is an ongoing process, one that requires constant learning. It's essential to understand that on our own and by our own strength, we will never be able to achieve it. The same goes for obedience. As Paul said, "For I have the desire to do what is good, but I cannot carry it out" (Romans 7:18). Everything depends on God's work within us. Our response is to open up our hearts, listen carefully, and act accordingly.

The unshakable foundation

Listening to the voice of God is an ongoing journey that unfolds with time and understanding. If you feel you've never heard directly from God or aren't certain if what you've heard is indeed the voice of God, it might be because God believes you don't need explicit directions in your current situation. Discerning God's calling is not about having an explicit instruction manual but rather becoming sensitive to the subtle stirrings of your heart as you learn more and more about God's heart. Our real challenge lies not in seeking affirmation of God's voice but in denying ourselves and listening humbly. As you listen, God will continually remind and guide you at the right time. Always keep your ears and heart open.

When it comes to our careers and ministries, God may not spell out the exact path to most Christians. But if your heart feels drawn towards a specific purpose or cause, that's likely where He's leading you. You don't need a glaring signpost from God for every choice you make. The specifics of the role or place aren't always the main focus. What's more important is recognising the purpose God has instilled in your heart and acting upon that knowledge.

We often get caught up in choosing specific positions or jobs, but this decision usually comes last. They are secondary. Many of my seminary students are worried about how to discern what ministry positions God is calling them to take. I often advise them not to decide too soon which church they should serve in; this isn't the most vital thing. What's more essential is knowing what kind of shepherds God wants them to be. The best position that aligns with their passions and burdens will become clear in due time.

Of course, prayer always plays a key role as we align our hearts with God's heart. We should rely on God to guide our decisions, and we also have the responsibility to go about and find the position that best suits us. But remember, roles can change too. Don't ask where God wants you to serve or what God wants you to do, but rather, focus on understanding the kind of person God wants you to become. Unless God offers you explicit guidance, you can act based on what you know and what God has put in front of you.

In our faith journey, the Word of God stands as the only objective foundation upon which we discern His voice. Each individual's relationship with God is deeply personal and unique, making it challenging to generalise or replicate. Consequently, our understanding of God is shaped by our personal experiences and beliefs, leading us to develop different theologies and experiences about Him. The crucial question, however, is whether these beliefs align with Scripture.

The Word of God serves as an unwavering benchmark in our faith. This highlights the importance of immersing ourselves in the study of Scripture, ensuring we approach God's Word with an open heart, without clouding it with personal biases. Our goal should be to allow Scripture to assess and refine our beliefs, ensuring they align with God's truth.

On the subject of spiritual encounters, many believers are drawn to supernatural experiences, sometimes placing them at the forefront of their faith journey. The Bible never encourages this, and it also warns us the Enemy may use signs and wonders to deceive believers.

If God sees a need for a specific miraculous experience in your life, He will surely provide it in His perfect timing and wisdom, whether you've sought it or not. Many have experienced this and have been profoundly transformed by deep encounters with God, showcasing the powerful work of the Holy Spirit in their lives. We must always remember: all spiritual experiences must be grounded in God's Word. The more profound the encounter, the greater the need to cross-check its alignment with the Word. We use Scripture to interpret our personal experiences, not the other way around.

Luke's transfiguration narrative serves as a poignant reminder in our journey of discerning God's calling. When the disciples stood on that mountain, amidst the dazzling spectacle, they grasped the voice but couldn't retain the experience. The dialogue between Moses, Elijah and Jesus highlights Jesus's imminent sacrifice and echoes his teachings of self-denial. Every individual, when heeding their divine calling, is called to carry their cross daily and follow him. The way forward is to anchor ourselves to God's Word, the unshakable foundation of our lives.

24

An alabaster jar and a new stone tomb

In my extensive conversations with Christians in Hong Kong over the years regarding the concept of calling, a common apprehension often emerges: that their talents, academic pursuits, or time invested in a particular profession might be in vain if these turn out to be different from God's calling for their lives. There is a subtle fear that lingers on – the possibility of wasting a career or untapped potentials – whenever Christians ponder their divine calling from God.

This question has been very personal to me, too. In 1972, as I completed my medical degree and began my medical career, I found my heart increasingly drawn to something else. A deep concern for the lack of quality biblical resources available for Chinese churches weighed heavily on my heart. Over the years, rather than fading, this burden only intensified. Eventually, my wife and I made a life-changing decision. We left our jobs and enrolled at Regent College in Vancouver, Canada. During my time there, God's guidance became increasingly clear to me. I wholeheartedly committed myself to the development of hermeneutics and biblical education resources for Chinese churches. My journey began when I joined the publishing department of China Graduate School of Theology (CGST) in 1980.

My decision to give up my medical practice raised some eyebrows. While some labelled it a waste, some Christians praised me for the sacrifice I made. But where is the waste, and where is the sacrifice? My medical training had certainly given me an investigative mind, which enabled me to examine Scripture analytically. My life has also been enriched abundantly by the learning and teaching experiences I have had at CGST.

I'm not saying all medical doctors should give up their profession. God has the final word in determining whether our lives and resources have been fruitful or in vain. After all, He is the one who calls us to be the person He has created us to be. The Bible sheds a lot of light on what is deemed wasteful and what is not in the eyes of God. In this chapter, we will explore the stories of two individuals who sacrificed something of immense value for Jesus, specifically for his burial. These stories challenge our understanding of value and waste, for God's criteria for assessing worthiness differs sharply from ours.

An unusual anointing

As the Gospel narratives draw close to the week preceding Jesus's crucifixion, the accounts focus more on Jesus's final words. Just before his death, Jesus would presumably have many important things to say to his disciples. Interestingly, the Gospel of Mark selectively reports only a few of Jesus's words, but he chooses to document two women who gave what they had: the poor widow (12:41–44) and the woman with the alabaster jar of perfume (14:3–9).

Both women offered something to God, and both received high praise from Jesus. The first gave a trivial amount, overlooked by others, while the second gave extravagantly, criticised by others as wasteful. Jesus defended them both. In this chapter, we'll look at the woman who anointed Jesus with an alabaster jar of perfume.

In Mark 14:3–9 we read:

> 3 While he was in Bethany, reclining at the table in the home of Simon the Leper, a woman came with an alabaster jar of very expensive perfume, made of pure nard. She broke the jar and

poured the perfume on his head.

4 Some of those present were saying indignantly to one another, "Why this waste of perfume? **5** It could have been sold for more than a year's wages and the money given to the poor." And they rebuked her harshly.

6 "Leave her alone," said Jesus. "Why are you bothering her? She has done a beautiful thing to me. **7** The poor you will always have with you, and you can help them any time you want. But you will not always have me. **8** She did what she could. She poured perfume on my body beforehand to prepare for my burial. **9** Truly I tell you, wherever the gospel is preached throughout the world, what she has done will also be told, in memory of her."

This woman's deep love for the Lord was evident. As she poured out the perfume, those around her immediately criticised her, complaining she had wasted a treasure. Had you been there and witnessed her action, the idea of "waste" might have crossed your mind as well.

But let's examine the heart of the matter: what does "waste" truly mean? By societal standards, her actions might not seem economically wise. The Bible underscores the value of the perfume she used – "pure nard", of unparalleled quality, unspoiled by any adulteration. In those times, this perfume was a luxury item, priced at more than thirty silver coins – roughly a year's earnings for an ordinary person. Pouring it all out in a single gesture might seem imprudent to many.

Yet, Jesus saw it differently. To him, it wasn't wasteful at all.

What really is "waste"?

I'd like to use an analogy to help illustrate this. Imagine a family with two sons. The elder is very gifted and becomes a professional with a high-paying job, while the younger struggles and takes up a low-paying job. How would you react if the elder brother is called by God to become a full-time pastor? Some might think, "It would have been better if God called his younger brother, who doesn't earn much. It's a pity the elder one has to give up his well-paid job."

Waste is in the eyes of the beholder and is rooted in our values. Waste, by definition, is using up something in an unworthy manner, resulting in a loss in value. In this analogy, people's judgement implies that the elder brother is more valuable than the younger, and that pastoral work isn't worthy for a person of such calibre.

How did Jesus respond to the people's criticism of the woman? He said, "Leave her alone. . . . Why are you bothering her? She has done a beautiful thing to me" (v. 6). In Jesus's eyes, the woman's action was anything but wasteful. This was because, as Jesus explained, she had done a "beautiful thing" for him.

The term 'beautiful thing' is rarely found in Scripture; the term 'good deed' is more common. Notably, 'beautiful thing' appears only a few times in the Bible, with at least two instances relating to giving to the poor (1 Timothy 5:10, 6:18). Jesus challenged the onlookers by questioning why giving money to the poor was considered worthy while offering it to him was seen as wasteful.

One might wonder whether Jesus really needed such a lavish gesture. Jesus's response provided a very important principle: anything done *for him* is not wasteful. Whatever you offer, whether much or little, as long as it's offered to the Lord, it isn't wasteful. This principle provides the benchmark by which we assess whether something is wasteful.

The original text of Mark 14:3–9 repeats the word 'have' four times. This is not conveyed fully in both the Chinese Union translation and the NIV. In Greek, 'have' means "to possess". The four instances are:

1. Verse 3: "A woman came with an alabaster jar of very expensive perfume." In the original Greek text, the woman *had* an alabaster jar of expensive perfume.
2. Verse 7: "The poor you will always *have* with you."
3. Verse 7: "But you will not always *have* me."
4. Verse 8: "She did what she could." In the original: "She does with what

she *has*", meaning she utilised all she had to its fullest potential. Both the Chinese Union and English NIV translations miss this.

The repetition of 'have' in the text is intriguing. We may have resources (like the alabaster jar) and people we need to serve (such as the poor), but we don't always have the opportunity to honour the Lord. While we might have visions, ministries and resources, what is in our hearts towards the Lord? When the opportunity arises, are we pouring out everything we have for the Lord or for ourselves?

An anointing with an eternal value

Jesus said:

> "She poured perfume on my body beforehand to prepare for my burial." (v. 8)

To understand the meaning behind Jesus's words, we need to first consider a particular cultural context. In Jesus's time, perfume served two primary purposes. First, it was used as a fragrance, much like the perfumes of today. The wealthy, during significant celebrations, would not hesitate to spend a fortune to anoint their hair with these precious ointments. Due to the warmth of the air indoors, the perfume would trickle down, reminiscent of the depiction in the Psalms where oil drips down to the beard (Psalm 133:2), filling the room with its aroma. Those who could afford it indulged in this lavish ritual without reservation.

The second use of the ointment was for anointing the deceased to prevent the body from giving off an unpleasant odour. For the Jews, the process of anointing the dead was of utmost importance. Jewish funerals were lengthy, and the deceased's body would be often accompanied by friends and family for several days. This anointing ritual, rich in aromatic scents, not only offered solace to the grieving family but also served as a final gesture of reverence and honour for the deceased. It gave them one last opportunity to serve and pay respect to the loved one, fulfilling a significant filial gesture.

Therefore, it was customary to meticulously anoint a body with a generous amount of perfume. However, the unique circumstances surrounding Jesus's death made this very challenging. Not only was his death right before the Sabbath, it also occurred during the annual Passover weekend. Scripture states that Jesus gave up his spirit at three in the afternoon, and Joseph of Arimathea promptly sought Pilate's permission to take Jesus's body in order to start the burial process. Since the Sabbath began at six in the evening, they had a very short time frame to complete the burial.

In the Gospels, throughout Jesus's life on earth, there were only two instances when Jesus was completely helpless and needed help from other people. On both occasions, someone came forward and offered him ointment. The first was shortly after his birth when the Magi from the east presented gifts of myrrh to the infant Jesus. The second time was at his death, when his body needed anointing. Although Nicodemus managed to anoint his body with myrrh and aloes (John 19:39), no one had the opportunity to honour him by pouring perfume on his body due to the timing of the Sabbath. Luke documents that some women, carrying spices, arrived at Jesus's tomb early before dawn after the Sabbath (Luke 24:1). They were desperate as they knew the anointing of Jesus's body had already been delayed by a couple of days. But by then, the tomb was empty, and Jesus had risen.

Hence, when Jesus said that the woman "poured perfume on my body beforehand", he meant that this act was a pre-emptive anointing, one that caught the right opportunity before Jesus's arrest and death. This opportunity should not be taken for granted because it would not happen again.

The woman herself probably didn't even realise that this would be the last opportunity to anoint Jesus before his death. Had she known that Jesus would soon depart from this world, she might have waited until after his death. Her love for Jesus was so profound that upon seeing him, she made the decision to pour out her entire jar of perfume on him.

Undeniably, if the perfume had been given to the poor, many people could have benefited. However, the act of pouring it all on Jesus totally transformed its meaning and significance. This woman poured out what she had. Jesus not only praised her act as a "beautiful thing", he also proclaimed that,

> "Wherever the gospel is preached throughout the world, what she has done will also be told, in memory of her." (v. 9)

An eternal legacy to the world

Jesus made a profound statement here. This woman, who was not even named by Mark, was to be remembered and honourably mentioned wherever the gospel is preached? What had she done that merited such a commendation from Jesus? Why did Jesus emphasise this? Jesus wasn't asking us to remember the woman herself, but to share the story of her actions – her sacrificial reverence for Jesus's sacrificial death.

The gospel, when preached, must persistently testify to Jesus's death on the cross, for he is the Lamb that God has prepared to die for the sins of the world once and for all. Every day, countless lives are lost worldwide, but only one death – Jesus's death – holds eternal significance for our salvation. The sharing of the gospel is not just mentioning Jesus's death, but also exalting and celebrating the ultimate significance of his death on earth. In the Jewish context, this act of honouring would be expressed through anointing the body with fragrant nard. Yet, only one person in history had ever managed to honour Jesus in this manner. Jesus saw her act not just as a simple act of anointing, but as a symbolic preparation for His burial. The profound meaning of her act might have eluded even her as she was simply offering her perfume to Jesus with utmost sincerity.

What Jesus values is this kind of heartfelt offering. The widow mentioned earlier (Mark 12) received Jesus's praise for the same reason. The economic value of her two small coins was almost nothing, yet Jesus declared her offering the most meaningful of all. The woman who poured out her jar of nard on Jesus, which was seemingly wasteful with no immediate practical benefit, was also given the highest praise by Jesus. Both gave all they had.

In the previous passage, Mark draws a sharp contrast between the widow and the religious leaders and teachers of the Law. Now, in chapter 14, who stands in stark contrast to this woman? Judas. As referenced in verses 10–11 of the same chapter:

> **10** Then Judas Iscariot, one of the Twelve, went to the chief priests to betray Jesus to them. **11** They were delighted to hear this and promised to give him money. So he watched for an opportunity to hand him over.

While the woman poured out her love and devotion to Jesus with everything she had, Judas appraised Jesus at a mere thirty pieces of silver. Mark meticulously details the actions of these two sacrificial women in the events leading up to Jesus's crucifixion, likely with the intent to underscore the paramount importance of a heart fully surrendered to God.

A short-lived burial with an eternal purpose

Now let's turn our attention to another individual who played a significant role in Jesus's burial. When we commemorate Good Friday and celebrate Easter Sunday, our focus often gravitates towards the crucifixion and then swiftly skips to the joyful climax of Jesus's resurrection. We tend to overlook one crucial intermediary event: Jesus's burial. To uphold Jesus's death and resurrection as historical truths, it was imperative that the details of what happened to Jesus's body be clearly recorded by eyewitnesses. The body would also need to be placed in a verifiable location, thereby ensuring the authenticity of eyewitness accounts of the empty tomb. Our faith today in our saviour's death and resurrection is firmly rooted in the Bible's detailed narration of these events.

All four Gospels document the process of Jesus's death and the events that followed. Apart from the historical figure of Pontius Pilate, another individual who was also mentioned by name in all four accounts was Joseph of Arimathea, for Jesus's body was obtained by him and buried in his tomb. Let's explore John's account (John 19:38–42) to learn more:

> [38] Later, Joseph of Arimathea asked Pilate for the body of Jesus. Now Joseph was a disciple of Jesus, but secretly because he feared the Jewish leaders. With Pilate's permission, he came and took the body away. [39] He was accompanied by Nicodemus, the man who earlier had visited Jesus at night. Nicodemus brought a mixture of myrrh and aloes, about thirty-five kilograms. [40] Taking Jesus's body, the two of them wrapped it, with the spices, in strips of linen. This was in accordance with Jewish burial customs. [41] At the place where Jesus was crucified, there was a garden, and in the garden a new tomb, in which no-one had ever been laid. [42] Because it was the Jewish day of Preparation and since the tomb was near by, they laid Jesus there.

As required by their customs, the Jews had to remove crucified bodies from the crosses before sunset (Deuteronomy 21:22-23). This concern would be especially serious before the Sabbath and the Passover. As Jesus died around three o'clock in the afternoon, they must secure Jesus's body from Pilate immediately in order to accomplish this.

This task posed significant challenges. Pilate, a Roman governor, was not particularly concerned with Jewish customs. It was the Jewish religious leaders who were anxious to avoid this religious taboo. Furthermore, due to the controversial nature of Jesus's death, anyone associated with him would risk being arrested. In this tense, politically and religiously sensitive atmosphere, who would have had the boldness and the cachet to approach Pilate and request Jesus's body? The individual daring to do this would also need to have the resources to handle and settle the body properly. Only a person of considerable social status and resources could achieve all of these in this tumultuous time.

Both Mark and Luke mention Joseph of Arimathea in prestigious terms as a council member, a role akin to that of a modern-day senator. This position presented practical challenges for him to display his faith in Jesus in public. So he might have come across as a timid, 'secret' believer who hesitated to openly profess his faith.

However, this perception doesn't align with the broader picture painted by Scripture. Both Mark 15:43 and Luke 23:50–51 portray him as a just and devout man who eagerly anticipated the kingdom of God. On at least one occasion, he took a bold stance in support of Jesus. As documented in Luke 23:51, when the council made the grave decision to arrest Jesus, Joseph strongly opposed their course of action, even when he was clearly outnumbered.

Although Joseph didn't openly declare his discipleship, this strategic position and decision served a purpose. When all of Jesus's public disciples had scattered in fear and gone into hiding after his death, Joseph the 'hidden' disciple boldly took advantage of his position on the Jewish Council and stepped forward to face Pilate. He was able to find favour in Pilate's eyes and successfully obtained permission to take Jesus's body.

God bestows advantages upon us in our lives not for our personal gain, but as instruments for His divine purpose. When God chooses to utilise the blessings He has granted us, we may be required to pay a price or summon the courage to step forward, much like Joseph. Joseph of Arimathea risked much by approaching Pilate and, as a result, accomplished what Jesus's disciples could not.

A unique tomb, a bold sacrifice

Another remarkable aspect of Joseph's involvement in the burial of Jesus was the provision of the tomb. While a tomb doesn't seem worthy of discussion, it holds profound significance in the context of Jesus's crucifixion. During that era, when a condemned individual was taken down from the cross, their body was often left on the ground, vulnerable to the threat of being scavenged by wild animals. In such a scenario, how could one provide evidence of a resurrection? This accentuates the critical importance of a secured and verifiable tomb.

However, at this moment, not only had Peter denied knowing Jesus three times, but the other disciples had also fled for their lives, leaving the responsibility of burying Jesus to others.

Securing an appropriate tomb for Jesus also presented a significant challenge. While our modern burial practices usually involve separate graves, Jewish ancient customs would place the deceased with their ancestors in big tombs that housed multiple family members. Only convicted criminals were excluded from this honour, necessitating individual burial. Jesus, due to the circumstances of his death, could not be laid to rest alongside others. The pressing issue was: where could a new tomb be found in under three hours?

The tomb had to be not only new but also nearby. The process of retrieving the body from the Roman authorities was time-consuming, and transportation only added to the delay. Therefore, it was essential for Jesus's tomb to be in close proximity to Jerusalem to ensure a timely burial. Joseph of Arimathea happened to have access to a new tomb nearby. While Arimathea was situated in the north, in a rural area where one would find a family tomb, Joseph's official duties in Jerusalem and his social status had allowed him to acquire an additional tomb. This particular tomb was close to Jerusalem, in a prime location, making it an exceedingly expensive tomb.

In addition to its prime location, the quality of Joseph's tomb was top-tier. The Bible deliberately highlights how this tomb was made: it was carved out of rock – a luxury only the very wealthy could afford. More crucially, this type of tomb had only one entrance without a back exit. Once the burial was completed, the entrance was sealed with a large stone. This was vital to ensure that no one could tamper with or steal the body.

Such tombs were very rare, and finding an empty one in just three hours was nearly impossible. Yet Joseph had access to such a rare and valuable asset, divinely prepared for Jesus. Before Jesus's death, Joseph couldn't have foreseen Jesus's need for his tomb. And he most likely had absolutely no idea about the significant purpose this asset would serve in history.

Perhaps the acquisition of this tomb was challenging for Joseph. Perhaps it was even more challenging for him to give it up. In this critical moment, he had to make a swift decision: to dedicate this tomb totally to the Lord or keep it for himself. Just like the woman's alabaster jar, there was no turning back. The bold sacrifice may have seemed wasteful to many, as the tomb could never be used again. Still, without hesitation, Joseph willingly offered his precious tomb for the Lord's use and promptly placed Jesus's body in it after retrieval.

Living out our calling

Imagine for a moment that you were in the same situation either as the woman with the alabaster jar or as Joseph. Could you do the same? Are you willing? God blesses us abundantly with various resources and gifts throughout our lives, yet we often cling to them tightly, afraid of losing out or missing out. We might ponder: is it worth it? What do I gain from it? What will others think? Will it be wasted?

We know that Jesus calls his disciples to take up their cross daily and follow him. But how do we practically live out this calling? The woman with the alabaster jar and Joseph provide us with exemplary models. They didn't hesitate for a moment to offer their precious possessions for the Lord's use when the opportunity arose. They were ever-ready to surrender the resources entrusted to them, holding nothing back.

Does God really need our love and resources? No. Does He need our help? Not really. He could command angels to do His work, with outcomes that would no doubt surpass our own. What we can do may seem limited or even insignificant. It's easy to underestimate what we can offer to God, thinking it may be trivial or lacking apparent practical value. What practical use could a jar of perfume and a tomb possibly have had for Jesus? However, when dedicated to the Lord with a sincere heart, God used them for His glory and purpose. There is no wastage in God. The alabaster jar and the tomb, offered wholeheartedly, have become the most unique and valuable gifts in human history.

God's calling for us, therefore, extends beyond choosing a career path, pursuing a university degree, or deciding which Christian ministry to serve in. It encompasses our dedicating every facet of our lives to God as a sacred offering, recognising that everything we possess is a gift from Him, given to us with a purpose for His glory. Nothing given to the Lord is ever in vain. Conversely, any aspect of our lives that remains withheld from God is wasted. God calls each one of us to love the Lord our God with all our heart, all our soul, all our mind and all our strength. Our response to this divine call should be to offer our entire lives in devotion. This is the essence of calling.

About the Author

Rev. Dr. Philip Yeung (Yeung Sek Cheung) was raised in Hong Kong and trained as a medical doctor at the University of Hong Kong. Five years into his practice, he believed God called him to leave his profession to serve in theological education in Hong Kong. His calling was to provide biblical teaching and training for Chinese church leaders, emphasizing the active integration of biblical knowledge with everyday life. After graduating from Regent College, Canada, with a Master of Christian Studies, he devoted the next 40 years of his life to teaching at the China Graduate School of Theology, where he specialized in the teaching of biblical languages, wisdom literature, as well as homiletics and pastoral care. His medical training, his proficiency in both biblical Hebrew and Greek, and his journey in discovering God's calling for his life, all equipped him with insights into the Bible as well as the ability to dissect biblical teachings and help his students apply them in modern life.

Over his four decades of ministry, Dr. Yeung developed a comprehensive theological framework known as Creation Theology, based on an analytical elaboration of the physical, functional and moral orders of creation as portrayed in Genesis 1-3. This framework became an integral part of his teachings on various aspects of Christian life, including vocation, spiritual formation, suffering, and the interpretation of wisdom literature in the Bible.

Dr. Yeung actively applied his Creation Theology framework in Bible studies, workshops and retreats. He was a frequent speaker at the Fellowship of Evangelical Students (FES, the Hong Kong branch of IFES), as well as the Hong Kong Professional and Executive Services (HKPES), a Christian organization focused on equipping Christians in the marketplace. His passion was to train university students and young Christian professionals, helping them to integrate their faith into their everyday work and life experiences.

Also by Dr. Philip Yeung

Jesus' Awkward Questions

Jesus asked many questions during his three years of ministry on earth, some provocative, some unsettling, and some rather strange! In Jesus' Awkward Questions, a medical doctor and Biblical Greek scholar dissects 12 stories where Jesus asked a peculiar question, and reflects on what Jesus was revealing about himself, the human condition, and how radically he speaks to our lives today.

Darkest Night, Brightest Dawn: A Lent Reflection

He who announced "I AM THE LIVING WATER" became thirsty; He who proclaimed "I AM THE RESURRECTION" entered death; He who promised "I WILL PREPARE A PLACE FOR YOU" was buried in a tomb; And he calls us to leave everything behind and follow him?

Dr. Philip Yeung leads us in a moving and radical journey of Jesus during the Holy Week, from the darkest hour at the hands of the betrayer to the brightest dawn at the empty tomb, and examines how unexpected details highlighted by the Gospel authors open our eyes to the unimaginable depth and length of God's love for us.